Come, Lord Jesus

Also by Tom O'Hara SJ
At Home with the Spirit
At Home with God
At Home with Jesus

Come, Lord Jesus

Contemplation and the Gospels

TOM O'HARA SJ

David Lovell Publishing
Melbourne Australia

Published in 2017 by
David Lovell Publishing
PO Box 44, Kew East
Victoria 3102 Australia
tel/fax +61 3 9859 0000
email publisher@davidlovellpublishing.com

© Copyright Tom O'Hara SJ 2017

This work is copyright. Apart from any use permitted under the Copyright Act 1968 no part may be reproduced by any process without written permission from the publisher.

Front cover: Christ and symbols of the four evangelists, stained glass window, St Peter's Church, in Peterslahr, Darstellung, photo by Reinhard Hauke.
Design by David Lovell Publishing
Typeset in 12/16 Hoefler Text
This edition printed through Ingram Spark

National Library of Australia Cataloguing-in-Publication data

O'Hara, Tom, 1932-2016.
Come, Lord Jesus : contemplation and the gospels / Tom O'Hara SJ.
ISBN: 978 1 86355 163 2 (paperback)
Jesus Christ. Ignatius, of Loyola, Saint, 1491-1556 *Exercitia spiritualia*.
Spiritual exercises. Contemplation.

248.3

Acknowledgements

Scripture quotations are taken from the New Revised Standard Version of the Bible © 1989, Division of Christian Education of the National Council of Churches of Christ in the United States of America.

'A Letter on the Interior Life' (pp. 209-2263) taken from *The Ladder of Monks and Twelve Meditations* by Guigo II, translated by Edmund Colledge and James Walsh, copyright 1981 by Cistercian Publications Inc., © 2008 Order of St Benedict, Collegeville, Minnesota. Used with permission.

Excerpt from the *The Spiritual Exercises of St Ignatius* (pp. 192-198), translated by Louis Puhl SJ (1951). Used with permission of Loyola Press.

Approved by the censor: Fr Robin Koning SJ

Foreword
Fr Frank Brennan SJ

Tom O'Hara SJ died on Tuesday 12 November 2916. His nephew, Frank Brennan SJ, concelebrated the Funeral Mass for Tom and delivered the homily. He has kindly agreed that the homily feature as the Foreword to this book. The homily was given at St Mary's Church, North Sydney, 17 November 2016.

Readings Hosea 11:1-4; Psalm 103, Romans 8:18-27, John 21:1-14

TOM STOOD HERE at this lectern, day in and day out for many years. He loved preaching, breaking open the word and reflecting on the challenges of life. He was always economical with his words, offering precise spiritual insights and accurate exegesis of the text. Consider his notes in his book *At Home with the Spirit* for the Gospel we have just heard:

> The disciples return to their Galilee homeland. They return to their community, but are still at a loose end. 'Let's go fishing.' It is in taking up their usual occupation that they meet the Lord.
> Enter into the scene: their straining to see the

mysterious figure through the mists on the shore. They help one another to recognize the Lord.

He comes to them according to their different personalities: to the clear-sighted 'beloved disciple', to Peter in his impetuous jumping overboard. Admire the exquisite hospitality of the risen Lord in barbecuing a fish for their breakfast. Fish, the symbol of Christian salvation.

There you have it: homeland, community, and being at a loose end; fishing, usual occupation, and the mystery; different personalities – clear-sighted, and impetuous; hospitality, barbecuing, and salvation. As Tom said in his introduction to *At Home with Jesus*, 'Our thirst for contemplative experience of our God can be satisfied in many ways, as God freely chooses to gift each of us. The way of God's choosing is through personal involvement with Jesus, the Son of God, revealed through the Gospel. The Word of God leads us into the deepest depths and up to the greatest heights of contemplation.'

As one of you put it: 'Fr Tom was sharply aware of the spiritual landscape, and used his wit to slash through it with love. *Ad Majorem Dei Gloriam*.' One of his grandnieces, hearing news of his death, texted me: 'Just opened a nice bottle and toasted Uncle Tom: eccentric, brilliant, not always attuned to social cues, but resilience in spades.' His extended family told it as it is. He'd have approved that.

Tom's life was encased by two bookends: bookends of untold grief and loss. His mum died when he not quite one. His dad died when he not much more than three. By then his Aunty Marg had come from Melbourne to Queensland to care for him and his older siblings Patricia and Frank. A decision was made that the three orphaned children would be brought up by different families at opposite ends of the country. Patricia and Frank remained in Queensland. The three-year-old toddler Tom travelled by boat with Aunty Marg from Brisbane to Melbourne

Foreword

to start a new life in South Melbourne, in the house built by his great grandparents who migrated from Ireland in 1864.

The second bookend was marked by his last trip a few months ago to the United Kingdom to visit his brother Frank and Frank's wife Hillary, and to visit his beloved Ireland one last time. In Ireland he hit his head badly and even took a photo marking what he described as the scene of the crime. On return, he had not a good word to say for Emirates airlines. He suffered a number of cerebral events.

Hillary died after a long illness with cancer. Then, on the Friday before last, Frank died of a massive heart attack. On the following Monday, Mum, Dad and I went to St Peter's Green to deliver the sad news of Frank's passing. Both Patricia and Tom, having lost much of their legendary cognitive capacities, embraced in their loss. On the Wednesday, we celebrated a simple funeral Mass for Frank in the St Peter's Green chapel. At the sign of peace, Tom greeted everyone individually and then embraced his beloved sister. At the end of Mass, a long-time North Sydney parishioner, now a co-resident at St Peter's Green and having no idea of Tom's condition, greeted him and thanked him profusely for his pastoral ministry here in the parish. Tom was overjoyed.

I then accompanied him back to the lock-up dementia ward where with delight he attempted to explain to his co-residents the sacramental celebration we had just shared. That evening he had a massive brain bleed and there was no point in surgery. He passed away on Saturday 12 November at midday – a week after his brother Frank had died, and just as the 3th General Congregation of the Jesuits was concluding in Rome with the new Superior General Fr Arturo Sosa telling us, 'Our faith in Christ, who died and rose, enables us to contribute with many other men and women of good will, to lay hands on a world that is sick and to help with its recovery.'

These two bookends provide the structure and the context for Tom's life of friendship and priestly ministry. He knew great loss and grief, but like Hosea he experienced God's tender love leading him with cords of human kindness and with ties of love. Like Paul, he considered that his sufferings were not worth comparing with the glory that will be revealed in us. Tom, more than most of us, had cause to groan inwardly waiting eagerly for adoption as a child through the redemption of his body. He knew that real hope was the hope in things that cannot be seen, hope in those things which have not been guaranteed by a safe, secure and nurturing family.

Interior freedom, abiding relationships with each other and with God, and commitment to the greater good were the hallmarks of the Ignatian spirituality he embraced in his teaching, in his writing, in his pastoral ministry, in his spiritual direction, in his preaching, and most particularly in his friendships. Having so little family life of his own, he embraced and enriched the family lives of so many of you gathered here today in such numbers.

I didn't get to know Tom until I was 12. Tom had just been ordained. He came to Queensland to visit the places of his lost family years – Toowoomba, Dalby and Jandowae. We travelled together in Dad's brand new Valiant. Once we got west of Dalby, Tom decided it was time to give this new car a test. He was thrilled when he reached 100 – and these were in the days of miles per hour. Being only 12, I had little sense of the enormity of emotions Tom must have been experiencing as we visited the places where his father had been the doctor and his mother a nurse.

For some years after that, the whole Brennan clan would travel to Sydney for Christmas holidays. We would stay at Manly, swim in the mornings, and then drive to Canisius College to fetch Tom before travelling over the bridge to Sacré Coeur Rose Bay to visit Dad's sister Mary. One day,

Foreword

when crossing the bridge, one of my younger siblings with a broad Queensland accent asked, 'Are we going to Rose Bay?' Reminiscent of George Bernard Shaw's Professor Higgins, Tom replied by contrasting an exaggerated Aussie twang with a most pukka accent, 'It's not Rose Bay, but Rose Bay.' On arrival in front of that large convent door at Sacré Coeur, we rang the bell and a fully habited sister answered. Before any adult could say anything, a young Brennan asked with the most refined accent imaginable, 'Is this Rose Bay?' Tom was delighted that his Sydney elocution and deportment lesson had born such fruit with such unrefined Queensland stock.

In early 1975, I had completed my university studies and was about to join the Jesuits. I took a student bus trip through Europe. In Rome, I met up with Tom who was studying and working there. We went for dinner. He chose the venue and I paid. It was one of the most expensive restaurants in Rome and I used up most of my traveller's cheques. Tom was completely oblivious. On my last night in Rome, he expressed shock that I had not visited the Jesuit Curia beside the Vatican. So at midnight we were on the steps of the Curia ringing the bell until someone answered. It was only years later when staying at the Curia that I realised how inappropriate this behaviour was.

Tom returned to Australia in 1976. From then on, he dedicated his life to the *Spiritual Exercises* of St Ignatius. He became an expert spiritual guide. He wrote accessible texts on the spiritual life including *At Home with God*, *At Home with Jesus*, and *At Home with the Spirit*. The titles carried the clue. Tom, who by any reckoning had started life with difficulty in finding a home and in being at home, found a home which he wanted to share – a home in the life of the Trinity furnished by the insights of Ignatius. And all the time, his spiritual insights were grounded in the practicality and earthiness of his life and of the lives of those whom he befriended, particularly through weddings and baptisms and here at regular celebrations of the parish Eucharist.

During the years on the parish team here at North Sydney, each day commenced with an early morning chat with John Yates who supervises the parish carpark – Tom drawing on his pipe and drinking from that filthy mug which was his constant companion on bushwalks and picnics. They would discuss the overnight sporting news and opine about the weather. Tom enjoyed dining in the flashest of homes and in the most basic of pubs – discussing any code of football or other sport, or alternatively Latin and Greek declensions and the outstanding unsolved clue of the morning's cryptic crossword. He assured us all that the Spirit helps us in our weakness.

He helped us to feel at home with our God. He had a knack of connecting with those at a loose end. He assured us, rich and poor, strong and weak, that we could meet the Lord in our usual occupations. He helped us recognise the mystery in life, celebrating the simplest of things, particularly sports, word games and magic of any sort. He was both clear sighted and impetuous, emulating the exquisite hospitality of his Lord especially with the annual barbecue for his married couples. Mind you, he expected to enjoy such exquisite hospitality in return when turning up on the doorstep unannounced or when setting out on those epic Corolla trips in January to Queensland. With his cap and his pipe, he was set to contemplate Christian salvation whether in the bush or at the back door of the presbytery.

Having often prayed, 'Take, Lord, receive all my liberty, my memory, understanding, my entire will', Tom is now at home with Jesus, at home with the Spirit, and at home with our God. May he rest in peace and may we continue to enjoy the exquisite hospitality of the Risen Lord here at the table of the Eucharist, content in knowing that the Lord will dispose of all we have and possess wholly according to his will.

Contents

Foreword Frank Brennan SJ   v

Introduction
Contemplation and the Gospels   1

Contemplating the Gospels
1. Contemplating the Trinity   25
2. Come, Lord Jesus   29
3. Prayer Is Infallible   33
4. Bartimaeus   37
5. In His Right Mind   41
6. Storm at Sea   45
7. Lazarus   49
8. Lenten Conversion   55
9. A Woman's Conversion   59
10. God, Be Merciful   63
11. Come on Down   67
12. Do Not Sin Again   70
13. Be Forgiving As Your Heavenly Father Is Forgiving   74
14. An Advent Contemplation   79
15. Go to Joseph   83
16. The Annunciation to Mary   87
17. Our Life of Hope   91
18. Jesus Is Baptized   95
19. Jesus Is Tempted   98
20. Jesus Goes Home   102

21. Happy the Poor in Spirit	106
22. The Birds of the Air	110
23. Feeding of the Multitude	114
24. Who Do You Say I Am?	119
25. You Are the Messiah	123
26. Jesus Is Transfigured	127
27. Lose Your Life	130
28. Preparing for the Passion	134
29. Gethsemane	138
30. He Is Risen	143
31. The Risen Jesus and Mary of Magdala	147
32. My Lord and My God	150
33. A Great Catch of Fish	154
34. I Am The Way	158
35. You Are My Friends	162
36. Life in Abundance	167
37. Father, Glorify Your Name	171
38. Safe from the Evil One	176
39. The Ascension	180
40. Come, Holy Spirit	184
41. Sacred Heart	188

Appendices

A. How Do I Contemplate a Gospel Mystery?	192
B. Contemplative Prayer	199
C. Excerpts from the *Spiritual Journal* of St Ignatius	203
D. A Letter on the Interior Life	209
Liturgical Settings for the Gospels	225

Introduction

Contemplation and the Gospels

IN HIS *SPIRITUAL EXERCISES*, St Ignatius of Loyola recommends to the retreatant to devote a good three quarters of the whole prayer enterprise to the contemplation of the mysteries of the Lord's infancy, public life, death and resurrection. Every time he writes about praying with the gospels, Ignatius uses the words 'contemplation' and 'mystery', unlike many later commentators on his *Exercises*, who replaced the words 'contemplation' and 'mysteries' with words like 'meditation' and 'events'. Ignatius never heard, of course, of phrases like 'Ignatian contemplation' or 'imaginative contemplation', which have come into vogue in recent years. Why are these phrases used? Often there is an implication that there is a necessity to distinguish between contemplation, as Ignatius understood it, and contemplation as understood by those who belong more to what is called the apophatic traditions of contemplation.

Theologians have been accustomed to distinguish between two different aspects of contemplative prayer, which they have named 'kataphatic' – involving thoughts, words, feelings – and 'apophatic' – involving the absence of thoughts, words and feelings. These are not two different forms of prayer but two aspects of the one prayer. All authentic contemplation involves both the kataphatic and the apophatic dimension. St Ignatius, like the great St Teresa of Avila, unashamedly emphasises the kataphatic dimension. Both dimensions are included in the broad term 'contemplation'. The Appendices in this book all direct their attention to the kataphatic aspects of prayer.

In Appendix A we have St Ignatius's account, from the book of the *Spiritual Exercises*, of how to go about contemplating the mysteries of the Lord in the gospels. In Appendix B, from *The Catechism of the Catholic Church*, there are nine definitions of contemplation. The very first one, from Teresa, is surprising in its simplicity, and liberating in its universality: 'Contemplative prayer is nothing else than a close sharing between friends; it means frequently to be alone with him who we know loves us.'

In Appendix C, brief excerpts from the *Spiritual Journal* of Ignatius for the period 8-28 February 1544, we see how Ignatius carried on the 'close sharing between friends' recommended by Teresa. Often in his prayer he sensed an immediate presence to God or to one of the Persons of the Trinity. When this didn't happen immediately, he would turn to his 'friends', whom he called his 'intercessors', namely Jesus and Mary. In the first of the excerpts of Ignatius we have these words, 'I desired to make this offering to the Father through the mediation and prayers of the Mother and the Son. First I prayed to her to assist me before her Son and the Father. Next I implored the Son that together with the Mother He might help me before the Father.'

From the first moments of his conversion at the age of thirty-one, Ignatius had a truly intimate relationship with Mary and with her son, Jesus. He conversed with them constantly, and invited those who followed his 'way of praying' to do the same. As we take up the outlines for contemplation developed in this book, we may do well to relate with the persons involved in each mystery. This applies to the Persons of the Trinity 'in whom we live and move, and have our being', to Jesus and to Mary, and to any saint (canonized or not) with whom we have a personal relationship. They are the friends with whom we are invited to have a close sharing in our prayer.

All contemplation begins from the natural gift of contemplation which is given by God to every person on the planet. Through this gift, we experience wonder, awe, surprise and intimacy, especially intimacy with other persons. Natural contemplation puts us in touch with the aspect of mystery in the thing, situation or person contemplated. We can well define natural contemplation as 'presence to mystery'. When one moves deeper into contemplation in contemplative prayer, the definition is expanded to 'presence in faith to mystery'. Contemplative prayer adds the dimension of faith, that is, personal relationship with God. The theological foundation of such prayer is established through our Baptism into union with ('in the name of') Father, Son and Holy Spirit.

Intimately linked to contemplation in the *Spiritual Exercises* is the great Benedictine way of praying known as *Lectio Divina* (Divine Reading). Of all the influences on Ignatius in his composing of the *Spiritual Exercises* none can rival the long hours he spent during his convalescence from a broken leg at Loyola in reading *The Life of Christ* written by the Carthusian, Ludolph of Saxony. Ludolph's work has virtually nothing in common with works with the same title by scripture scholars of the 19th and early 20th centuries, in which they attempted to recapture 'the historical Jesus'. It is the fruit of his *Lectio Divina* which he invites his readers to participate in ceaselessly, day and night.

Appendix D is the classic work on *Lectio Divina* by the 13th century prior of La Grande Chartreuse, Guy the Second, entitled 'A letter on the interior life', sometimes known as *The Ladder of Monks* (*Scala Claustralium*). In it we see the fruits of Guy's own 'divine reading' in his unceasing references to the gospels, the psalms and other scripture texts. This same feature of repeated quotation of scripture, and of the Fathers of the Church, abounds in Ludolph's *Life of Christ*.

The main advance on the writing of Ludolph made by Ignatius is his emphasis on the imagination. This is the faculty intimately bound up with personal relationship. The personal relationships of our lives are carried in our imagination and become activated whenever we re-enter them in the use of that faculty. Through our imagination we are present to the risen Lord who is always present to us. In our Prayer we may use our imagination in multiple ways, but the key factor is that imagination ushers us into an authentic divine presence. Correctly, for Ignatius, Prayer is personal relationship with God in Christ. There is no Prayer apart from relationship, as is clearly illustrated in our excerpts from the *Spiritual Journal* of Ignatius (Appendix C). Sometimes people refer to 'relational prayer', as if there were any other kind. 'Relational prayer' is the ultimate tautology.

Contemplation is a dimension of all true prayer, rather than a different way of praying. Without this dimension, vocal prayer would be just reciting empty words, and meditation would be just thinking holy thoughts. In reality both vocal prayer and meditation lead us into contemplation.

Besides our definition above, there are many terms to describe contemplation, such as 'silent love' (John of the Cross) or 'prayer of the heart'. A very helpful distinction is that of the author Gérard Fourez, calling Prayer with a capital 'P', 'a profound attitude of heart in God's presence', and prayer with a small 'p', 'an activity by which we try to cultivate Prayer'. The 'profound attitude of heart in God's presence' is indeed contemplation.

Since Vatican II, praying with Scripture, previously a rarity among Catholics, has become commonplace. The result is a renewal and deepening of contemplative life for many people. When we take up the Scriptures to pray, the obvious place to start is with the gospels. When we do this, two complementary elements come into play: first, opening our heart to the Word which speaks to each one personally in the power of the Spirit, communicating to each the Christ-life it contains; second, a growing knowledge and appreciation of what the gospels are and how to use them most profitably. Clearly the first element is the more important, but the second has its significance.

Contemplation and the Gospels

An obstacle to our praying with the gospels is the misunderstanding that the four evangelists were interested in writing a biography of Jesus, a history of his life and times, in the sense that we understand history today. For them, the chronology and geography of his life were very secondary, and could be treated with great freedom in accordance with their essential purpose, which is theological and spiritual. Each of the gospel writers in his own way sets out to tell us who Jesus is: not so much who Jesus was when he walked our earth, but who is he is for the writer and his community. The gospels are essentially stories about the risen Christ, who was operative in the lives of the Christian communities at the time they were written, meeting their needs. The same risen Christ is at work in each of our communities today, meeting our needs.

Once we have grasped this basic understanding of a gospel, we are liberated from the old 'harmony' mentality, the attempt to make one continuous, coherent 'life of Christ' out of what are four different works, each inspired by the Holy Spirit, and each to be respected in its own unique individuality. Instead of throwing the four gospels into a melting pot, we have four presentations of who Jesus is, each of them enriching our personal relationship with him.

The Spirit who inspired the gospels was well aware that no one written word could capture the infinite variety of the face of Christ, so we have four different portraits. In so far as we are in touch with each of them in its distinct individuality, our whole relationship with the Lord grows richer. It is somewhat like our way of using different artistic representations of Jesus. We can contemplate the Lord, as the artist intended, with the help of a Byzantine icon. We relate differently in contemplating a Renaissance work, like the crucifixion by Guido Reni. We can have a third experience of the Lord in contemplating a modern work like that of Georges Rouault. We have no photograph of

Jesus, but the diversity of portraits enriches our contemplation of him in ways that no photograph could.

An awareness of whether it is the Jesus of Mark, Matthew, Luke or John can be a great help, as we shall see later, but the first essential for our contemplation is that I be present to him as the passage I have in hand reveals him to me. There are many ways that the passage I have chosen may touch me. It may lead me to reflect on my life, offer me healing or forgiveness, console me, call me, challenge me – the possibilities are endless. But the basic power of the Word is to bring me into the presence of the risen Lord who is drawing me into closer relationship with the Father through the Spirit.

In its first document, that on the sacred liturgy, the Second Vatican Council expanded the previously accepted understanding of the words 'real presence'.

> Christ is always present in his church, especially in her liturgical celebrations. He is present in the sacrifice of the Mass, not only in the person of his minister, 'the same one now offering himself through the ministry of priests who formerly offered himself on the cross', but especially in the Eucharistic species. By his power he is present in the sacraments, so that when anybody baptizes it is really Christ himself who baptizes. He is present in his word, since it is he himself who speaks when the holy scriptures are read in the church. Last, he is present when the church prays and sings, for he has promised 'where two or three are gathered together in my name, there am I in the midst of them' (Matthew 18:20)' (*Sacrosanctum Concilium*, par. 7).

It is precisely the presence of the risen Lord in his word that enables us to be present to him, to have a real encounter with him when we take up the gospels in prayer.

Prayer is a personal meeting with God. This meeting takes

place in, with and through Christ. We meet Christ in the Gospel. The gospels are the Good News of the risen Lord active in our lives today. We meet him today. We grow in faith, in hope, in love, in trust, in friendship whenever we read and ponder the words of the gospels. The daily reading of the gospels puts the reader in touch with the Lord Jesus. This is why praying the gospels is such an important prayer for a Christian. The greatest gift we have from God is our Baptism, leading, of course, to its climax in the Eucharist. Through Baptism we receive the gift of the Spirit of the risen Lord Jesus, making us one with him. The same Holy Spirit cries out in our hearts, '*Abba!* Father!' (Romans 8:15; Galatians 4:6). This leads Paul to the paramount truth of our adoption as sons and daughters of the Father.

The essence of our personal relationship with Christ is nowhere better proclaimed than in the great text of Paul in Romans 8:29: 'We have been chosen by God to be conformed to [literally, 'shaped with'] the image of God's Son.' This conformation is clearly not physical but spiritual, as we put on the mind and heart of Christ, and mystical, as we live out in our own lives our profound union with him.

Here we have the theological roots of all Christian contemplation. For all the great mystics, contemplation is that gift of prayer that wells up from within. If we are authentically present to the Jesus of the gospels, we are not just exercising our imagination, but are contemplative in the strictest sense of the word. Nothing in Christian contemplation can ever go beyond the contemplative doctrine of St Paul and St John.

To be contemplative is to be at home with Jesus, as in John chapters 14 to 17. 'If anyone loves me and keeps my word, my Father will love them, and we will come to them and make our home in them' (John 14:23). 'Make your home in me, as I make my home in you' (15:4). 'If you remain in me and my words remain in you, you may ask what you will and you will get it' (15:7). 'Father, may they be one in us, as you are in me and I am in you. With me in them and you in me, may they be completely one' (17:21-23). Or, in the first letter of John, 'Those who live in love live in God, and God lives in them' (1 John 4:16). Paul has the same contemplative theme of living: 'I live, now not I, but Christ lives in me' (Galatians 2:20). 'For me, to live is Christ' (Philippians 1:21).

In his first model of contemplation of a gospel mystery in the *Spiritual Exercises* (see Appendix A), St Ignatius invites us to enter into deliberation with the Persons of the Trinity as they plan the Incarnation for the salvation of all on planet Earth. In other words, the person contemplating in the twenty-first century is to participate with the Trinity in bringing about universal salvation. This is truly a model for all contemplation of the Gospel. The subject for contemplation is Salvation History. Ignatius never intended that we leave behind this contemplation and move on to something else. Every mystery of the Christ of the gospels gives expression to the Mystery of the Trinity's saving work in Christ, It is that same Mystery that is being accomplished in the lives of each of us today. As we contemplate the gospels, we insert ourselves firmly into the stream of Salvation History. Through relationship to the Persons of the Trinity and to the realities of our world we participate in the here and now work of redemption.

What we do in contemplation is to appropriate in prayer and implement in our living the grace already present in the Gospel. The gifts expressed above by John and Paul are given to all the baptized through the indwelling of the Holy Spirit. That Spirit is the Spirit of the risen Lord, the Jesus with whom we are put into living, personal contact whenever we take up the gospels. Through our contemplation we appropriate the grace of our baptism, so that it becomes more effective in its influence on the whole of our living – our thoughts and feelings, both conscious and unconscious, all our actions, even our bodies. We are gradually being transformed in fact into the 'other Christs' we already were truly, but potentially. Now that potential is being realized.

In this sense we are all called to be mystics. This is not some revolutionary modern teaching. As long ago as 1926, Dom Cuthbert Butler concluded his classic work *Western Mysticism* by writing, 'We learn that mysticism, like religion itself, is within the reach of all. It is not too hard for you, nor is it far off. It is not in heaven, that you should ask, who will go up to heaven to bring it down for us? It is very near to you, in your mouth, and in your heart, that you may do it.' In the final quotation, Butler is applying to mysticism the words of Deuteronomy 30:11-14.

In a more recent work (*Mystical Theology*, 1995) William Johnston refers to the universal call to mysticism expressed by Bernard Lonergan: 'The original and almost shocking thing in Lonergan is that he looks on mystical love as the goal and climax of human living. This love is the peak-point of the thrust towards self transcendence and authenticity that is rooted in the minds and hearts of all human beings. There is nothing elitist about it. It is not a gift offered to Christians alone. It is not offered to religious people alone. It is offered to all men and women who would be fully human. Can we not conclude that for Lonergan there is a universal call to mysticism?' William Johnston himself had espoused the same position several years earlier in his book *Being in Love* (1988) where he wrote, 'Mystical contemplation is not extraordinary, it is very ordinary. All Christians, I believe, are called to it; and when they follow this path, they become their true selves, their very ordinary selves.'

If we start our contemplation with the gospel of John, we are immediately plunged into the heart of the mystery of the Trinity, the Word who is God dwelling with God from all eternity. The only Son whose reality moves into the bosom of the Father (John 1: 18) shares with us God's life. Through his story of the 'beloved disciple' who reclined on the bosom of

Jesus at the Last Supper John indicates that every disciple is to move with Jesus into the bosom of the Father. The beloved disciple remains anonymous for John as the type of every Christian disciple. This has always been recognized in Christian tradition in its understanding of the giving of Mary to be the mother of us all when Jesus, on the cross, entrusted her to the beloved disciple (John 19:26-27).

If we commence with Matthew or Luke, we are first invited to a loving presence to the Person of God-with-us or Salvation for the People, who is present in our world, not in word or thought or action, but in the form of an infant. If we turn to Mark, we are present to the mystery of the Good News of God's Son (Mark 1:1), revealed first in his Baptism. As we follow the dynamic of any of the four gospels, we are progressively challenged to deeper and deeper levels of contemplation.

We are called to be engaged with Jesus in his ministry of teaching and healing, leading us always on to the mystery of the Eucharist, symbolically presented in the form of the feeding of the five thousand. Mark and Matthew link this great Eucharistic symbol to the striking nature miracle of walking on water, as the preludes to the great question Jesus poses 'Who do you say that I am?' Luke, in a famous 'omission' of much of Mark's material, goes straight from the feeding to the great question (Luke 9:18). For John, the great question, in the form, 'Will you too go away?' (6:67), is in an even more explicit Eucharistic setting (John 6:1-58). Mark, in 7:14-27, has Jesus ask the disciples no fewer than nine times if they have managed to penetrate contemplatively the mystery of those actions of his that reveal his identity.

Clearly, the great question itself is not seeking an intellectual answer but a contemplative answer coming from the heart of each one. Immediately after Peter's response to the question of Jesus, the challenge to a radical new depth is proposed. Can they take on board the sayings about discipleship and the cross? These sayings cannot be comprehended by mere human reasoning. It is only in contemplation in union with Jesus that we can enter into the mystery of losing our life in order to find it. Closely linked to the prediction of sufferings is the great scene of the Transfiguration, once again inviting our contemplation.

When we come to the Lord's Passion itself, we are invited again to a new level of deeper contemplative prayer; all we can do is to stay with him in profound silence. This is the only way into the faith of the Roman soldier who proclaimed, when he saw how Jesus died, 'Indeed this man was God's son' (Mark, 15:39). Finally, in the resurrection we are called upon to meet the Lord who is truly hidden in every aspect of our material creation. It is only the truly contemplative who can penetrate this hiddenness.

The Word of God contains within itself the power to touch our hearts. That power is at its best when we are present to the person and message of Jesus of the gospels. This sense of presence is often revealed in our imagination. The gospels are each written in a style that is simple, concrete and imaginative. They are full of carefully crafted stories and powerful dramas which have the power to draw the reader into the action. When we read them carefully, slowly and attentively, it is not difficult to feel involved in what is taking place. I may form a visual image of Jesus and others involved in the scene. I may feel him touch me or hear him speak to me. More importantly, I have a sense of presence and relationship. This may not be clearly definable, but all my previous experience of him comes to life in my unconscious. Theologically, my baptismal relationship with him, with the Holy Spirit and with the Father is activated and becomes more operative in my life.

Jesus is truly our brother. There is a deeper reality here, taking us further into the mystery. He and I are one. Now, while this oneness is an objective fact, it needs to be developed, to grow, to come alive in me. This is where a life of personal contemplation comes in. Through my contemplation, I am present to the Christ-life within. I am in touch with the Lord. He is the same Lord Jesus who walked the roads of Palestine. The gospels reveal to us the truth of Jesus's life on Earth; but they are far more than this. They are a communication of the here and now life of the risen Lord. As I pray the gospels, I don't merely learn about a Jesus who lived a long time ago. I grow to be more like Jesus who is alive today: in all of creation, in all events, in all persons, in me!

The essence of our personal union with Jesus is nowhere better expressed than by Paul in the great text of Romans 8:29: 'For those whom he foreknew, he also predestined to be conformed to the image of his Son, in order that he might be the first of many brothers.' We have been chosen by God to be conformed to [literally, 'shaped with'] the image of God's Son in mind and in heart. The mystical prayer of contemplation of Christ in the Gospel is what perfects in us God's work of shaping us into the image of God's Son.

The truth which the Scriptures reveal to us is, in the words of Vatican II, 'that truth which God wanted put into the sacred writings for our salvation'. While the gospels give us an historical setting and outline of the life of Jesus, they have very little interest in history as we understand it today. The gospels contain far more story than history. While history speaks to our intellect, stories touch and fire our imagination. As we ponder the gospels, our hearts are formed and shaped by the personality and inner life, the heart, of the Lord. This takes place via our imagination. Imagination here is not understood simply as the power to form inner sense images apart from external stimuli. Imagination opens to us the world of symbol, of deep feeling, of presence to another, of personal relationship.

Unfortunately our education has tended to play down imagination. We were taught to believe that what is most real is what is materially most solid. Dreams and visions were often dismissed as 'only imagination'. The truth is the reverse. Imagination is far more real than steel and concrete. It is more real because it puts us in touch with what is truly and fully human. In our imagination we are inspired and challenged. We dream dreams that lead us to go beyond our limitations to live in reality the kind of life Jesus lived.

The value of imagination in the Christian life is made especially clear in the stories of the birth and infancy of Jesus in the gospels of Luke and Matthew. John introduces his gospel with the famous prologue in the philosophical-theological language of 'the Word'. Luke and Matthew communicate who Jesus is by telling us beautiful, pictorial, imaginative stories. Luke's primary message is that Jesus is 'salvation for all the peoples'; Matthew's message is that he is 'God-with-us'. They don't simply write these truths, but they fill our minds with images of angels, shepherds, the Temple, journeys, dreams, kings, wise men, precious gifts. As we fill our imagination with these symbols, the gospel truth is communicated to us on the deep level of the heart.

In what sense can I be present in prayer today to the Jesus who lived 2000 years ago? Perhaps I am a great admirer of Pope John XXIII. I remember what he looked like, his smile, what he said, his tone of voice, in fact the whole quality of his personality. I still know him. Death does not destroy authentic personal relationships. The same can be true of great historical figures or saints from eras even long gone, about whom I have read. The same is true of Jesus. The Spirit operates in, with and through the human, and in, with and through this human way of relating.

In 2012 a veteran of the Coral Sea battle takes the opportunity on the fiftieth anniversary to revisit the scene of that battle, which was decisive in the defence of Australia from Japanese invasion. He goes already armed with a cluster of memories. But, as soon as he arrives at the scene, more memories and images flood in. In imagination he sees again the position of the ships, the faces of his comrades, the bombs dropping through the air, the exploding vessels. He hears the sound of it all. He touches again his dying friend whom he'd held in his arms. He grasps again the hands which reached out to pull him from the water. He smells the explosives, the dead bodies, and tastes again the sweat, blood and tears. Many feelings are aroused in him. He experiences great emotion. He weeps again. But he experiences being carried beyond imagination and emotion into deeper feelings, like loss, grief, gratitude and love. He knows that he has entered into his heart, and remains a long time in profound silence. This experience will remain with him always and influence him for the rest of his life.

Here we have a striking example of the exercise of the natural gift of contemplation. We may ask whether, as our friend exercised this gift, the Coral Sea battle took place again. The stock answer is that objectively it did not, though subjectively for him it did. Yet there is a real sense in which the historical event is not simply past. He has relived through entry into contemplation something that has retained its existence as it has passed into eternity.

When we come to contemplate a mystery of the life of Jesus in the gospels, all of the kinds of things that our man experienced in his Coral Sea contemplation may happen to us. Grace truly builds on nature. Our contemplation in prayer takes place in, with and through the natural gift of contemplation. Yet there is something more here. In presenting the contemplation of the Incarnation St Ignatius suggests that we be present to the Word who has just become incarnate for us. The perfect tense points us to the enduring presence of a past event, as in the threefold acclamation at the Eucharist: Christ has died, Christ is risen, Christ will come again. Christ died, but his death has effectively just happened now. Notice that we do not say 'Christ is dead.' His death has occurred, but is not simply over and done with.

Can we go further? Yes, we can. All the events of history have an eternal quality about them. There is the obviously discernible effect of the past: I am a result of my history; 'the child is father to the man'. But over and above this, there is an abiding, eternal dimension to every human event. In the case of the Lord Jesus this is infinitely heightened through his Resurrection. Every event of his earthly history becomes eternally present through the transforming power of the Resurrection. This is why the author of the Book of Revelation writes of the Lamb that was slain now standing in the presence of the throne (Revelation chapter 5). The events of the earthly life of Jesus have gone forward into glory through the power of the Resurrection. As the author of Hebrews puts it, 'Jesus Christ is the same yesterday, today and forever' (Hebrews 13:8).

The evangelists convey the same truth when they have Jesus display his wounded hands and feet (Luke 24:39) and even his side (John 20:27). This is why the evangelist John can legitimately present the Passion and Death of Jesus as an activity of the risen Lord. Jesus goes forth in power to his suffering and death, and from the cross he hands over the Spirit. John is able to bypass a three-day wait for Resurrection, and a fifty-day wait for the sending of the Spirit.

Does this mean that, over and above their enduring presence, the events of the life of Jesus are actually happening now? It is totally correct to speak of Jesus suffering now in his suffering members. But this does not mean that Jesus himself is suffering: 'The death he died he died to sin, once for all, but the life he lives he lives to God' (Romans 6:10). Contemplation takes place from the perspective of eternity. When I contemplate, I am in touch with the risen Lord in his mysteries. They are called 'mysteries' from the Greek verb 'to hide', because they have a hidden or deeper meaning.

So, as I pray in union with this risen Lord, the historical events of the life of the Lord are taking place within the perspective of this prayer. Yes, from the point of view of the praying person, he is being scourged now. This is why my experience of compassion or grief is not just some voluntaristic exercise in which I step outside of present reality to pretend that something essentially past is in fact happening before my eyes. There is far more involved than a fanciful reconstruction through imagination of an event that remains essentially past. For me, as I pray, it is *happening*. This is amply confirmed in practice. Without the benefit of this theoretical understanding, this is precisely the experience reported again and again by persons contemplating the mysteries of Christ as they make the full *Spiritual Exercises*.

The only facts concerning the childhood of Jesus that Luke and Matthew have in common are the names of his parents, the virginal conception, that he was born in Bethlehem and grew up in Nazareth. They are far more interested in firing our imagination than in satisfying our curiosity. As we ponder the gospels, the same principle applies to the geography as to the history. It is not necessarily a help to the fruit of our contemplation to have visited Israel. We picture the scene in whatever way we wish. Nor do we have to be another Michelangelo. The 'pictures' can be extremely vague; what matters is our sense of presence.

As we pray the gospels in our imagination, we are doing what St Paul urges the Philippians to do: 'Whatever is true, whatever is honourable, whatever is just, whatever is pure, whatever is lovely, whatever is gracious, if there is any excellence, if there is anything worthy of praise, fill your minds with these things' (Philippians 4:8).

Whenever we read the stories of any great historical or fictional character, we form in our imagination a relationship with that person. We may see them, more or less clearly; we can may hear the sound of their voice; but the essential thing is that we truly relate with them. The mention of their name evokes a whole series of associations that we have built up in our imagination. The gospels, like any great drama or biography, have the power to touch us in this way. They have an additional, far greater, power because they are not just human words but God's Word.

The central character, Jesus, is not just a great man. He is the Lord, alive and well today. He and I are one through Baptism, and through the Eucharist. So I don't just read about him. He speaks in my heart and relates to me from within the deepest part of my person. The Jesus of the Gospel is the same Jesus who is alive 'in all things' now (Colossians 3:11). He is the same Jesus who is already at the end of history, drawing the whole of it and all of us together into himself and so into the Father (see 1 Corinthians 15:28).

With this background in mind, we take up the gospels as the special way of growing in that intimacy with Jesus which we call faith. We begin with a prayer to grow in this faith and intimacy. It is the prayer of the musical *Godspell* – to see thee more clearly, to love thee more dearly, to follow thee more nearly, day by day. The history of this little prayer goes back through St Ignatius to the English saint, Richard of Chichester (13th century). After making this prayer, I begin to open my inner self to the Gospel and to Jesus whom it reveals. The simplest, most obvious and most helpful way to start to do this is by using my five senses. The senses are the faculties through which we have an immediate presence to reality.

Can I see Jesus? Some texts of the gospels may be especially good for this kind of prayer. For instance, in the fourth chapter of Luke, Jesus stands up to read and 'all eyes were fixed on him' (verse 20). These words may help me to focus my imagination on seeing Jesus. I may allow myself to be 'amazed at the gracious words that come from his lips' (verse 22). Or I may find it easy to see him in the crib of Bethlehem, or being carried by his parents up to the Temple for the Presentation, or walking the Galilean countryside, or getting into a boat. Whatever the particular gospel scene, it is important to delay for a while to try to be with Jesus in my imagination.

The intimate knowledge of Jesus for which we asked at the start of our prayer is a 'heart knowledge'. It begins with my sense of being in his presence as I contemplate the gospel passage. Through this presence relationship grows. I become more like Christ, not in a sort of external imitation of him, but in putting on his mind and heart. I don't have to be working out in my head what the gospel is saying to me. It is sufficient to rest in the Lord's presence. He is his message. If I am truly in touch with him, I am really hearing the gospel message.

During this kind of praying with the gospels, I touch the Lord, just as he touched the leper in Mark 1:41, or as the penitent woman touched his feet in Luke 7:38. At Bethlehem I ask Mary if I may nurse the baby! I can also use the senses of taste and smell in a contemplative way. 'Taste and see that the Lord is good' (Psalm 34:8). 'Your robes are all fragrant with myrrh and aloes and cassia' (Psalm 45:8). The life of the Lord enriches the whole of my personality, including each one of the five senses. This kind of prayer gives me a sense that I have been in the presence of the Lord, and my life is being gradually transformed by the Word, in both its meanings, the Gospel and the Word-made-flesh.

The Scriptures continually instruct us to listen to God's Word. See the great prayer of Israel in Deuteronomy 6:4, or the words of Isaiah 55:2-3, and the constant references in all four gospels to hearing Jesus and listening to his words. I commence by listening carefully and attentively as I read the words. But it is important to go deeper; to allow the Word to sink in, to go down to that level understood by the word 'contemplation', where it is not so much the meaning of the words that nourishes my mind, but a taste for the Word which nourishes my heart. By constantly repeating in prayer the words of the gospels, I can learn them by heart. Then perhaps they well up from my unconscious at times when the Lord wishes to enlighten my daily life with the light of his Gospel.

As we continue to be present to the Lord Jesus through exercising the senses of our imagination, we grow in the grace of heart knowledge, of love and of intimacy that we asked for at the start of our prayer. The more we allow this to happen, the more we are prepared for a mystical experience of that presence, love and intimacy. It is only right to expect this to happen at least occasionally. In this kind of mystical experience the inner senses of the imagination are overtaken by the 'spiritual senses'. Throughout the tradition of Christian mysticism, these spiritual senses have been regarded as the human faculties used by God to communicate directly with the person at prayer. Nowhere is the teaching expressed more richly than by the great Franciscan, St Bonaventure:

> The soul believes in, hopes in, and loves Jesus Christ who is the incarnate, uncreated, and inspired Word, 'the Way, the Truth and the Life' (John 14:6). When by faith one believes in Christ, the uncreated Word and Splendour of the Father, the believer receives the spiritual sense of hearing and seeing: hearing the words of Christ and seeing the splendour of his light. When one desires the inspired Word, one recovers a spiritual scent through such desires and affections. When one embraces the Incarnate Word in love, receiving thereby light and ecstatic love from Christ, the lover has recovered spiritual taste and touch. Thus, with the spiritual senses reinvigorated, one can see, hear, smell, taste and embrace the Spouse (*The Mind's Road to God*).

Over and above the sense of presence, we have the fact that Jesus speaks and acts in a way that proclaims a set of values, the Gospel values. Praying with the gospels brings home to me the love, courage, compassion, openness of Jesus, his thirst for justice and solidarity with the poor. I am challenged by the conditions of discipleship: the grain of wheat must fall into the ground and die. I am drawn to know and accept that I must follow him all the way to my own Calvary and my own Resurrection.

As we pray with the gospels, we come more and more deeply into the presence of the Lord Jesus. We are not merely reading the gospels as we would read another book, to 'learn something', to 'discover the message'. We are present to a Person. We are present on the level of heart to heart. We are present to the Lord with whom we are already one.

While this truth is basic and must always be at work as we contemplate the Lord in the gospels, true Christian contemplation will never transport us into some heavenly, 'spiritual' world out of touch with the realities of our human life in the third millennium. The words of author Marshall McLuhan, 'The medium is the message', are eminently true of the Lord. We hear his message in being simply present to his person. At the same time it is necessary to reflect on the teachings of the gospels and apply them to our own lives. An outstanding aspect of those teachings, which we must never overlook, is that of ceaseless devotion and work for justice in a preferential option for the Lord's poor.

The Lord of the Gospel speaks in very clear terms to each person today who is willing to undertake the adventure of being open to his call. Some Gospel truths are basic to the life of every one of us. We are all called to be empty of self, as the Lord was (see Philippians 2:5-11). The Christian must be like Jesus, 'the man for others'. For all of us he proclaims the greatest commandment – love of God with our whole heart and of our neighbour as ourselves. We must even love our enemies. The way of the Gospel is the way of Jesus, the way of poverty of spirit. To be poor in spirit is to accept the whole reality of our humanness, our gifts and our shortcomings, strengths and weaknesses, joys and sorrows. Gospel persons do not try to escape from any aspect of life, or to anaesthetize or distract themselves from difficulty, pain and struggle. They embrace and celebrate their humanness to the full.

Every Christian must follow the Lord in rejecting the temptations to wealth, power and self-aggrandizement, and follow instead the way of spiritual poverty, service and humility. The Beatitudes give us the 'Charter of the Kingdom', which we are all called to live. In so far as we respond to their challenge and live by them, we receive God's blessing and find true happiness at the heart of self-sacrifice. The only way for any of us to join this kingdom is the way of the little child. Every Christian must take up the cross daily and follow Christ. 'Those who try to save their life will lose it; those who lose their life for my sake will find it.' This is the only saying of Jesus which appears in all four gospels. It is found twice in Matthew and twice in Luke, so six times in all. It must be the essence of the Gospel message!

As we pray daily with the gospels, we 'put on the Lord Jesus Christ' (Romans 13:14; see also Galatians 3:27). This happens in the depth of our heart, more or less unconsciously, through contemplation. At the same time, we become consciously more aware of fundamental Christian values as suggested in the previous paragraph. There is a third level of conversion that must also be attended to. Not only must I strive to say 'Yes' to the universal demands of Gospel values, but I must reflect carefully upon my own life to see how the Lord's message needs to be applied to all of the varying details of my life today.

One of the healthiest movements in modern prayer is that of being free to express in our prayer exactly how we feel. We are encouraged to be more like the psalmist, who complained to God, became impatient and angry with God, and never tired of pouring out to God the details of what was going on in his life. In this way our prayer becomes more real. Through our modern education, means of communication and the media, every one of us is in touch with a vast network of complex realities that make up our lives. We bring into our prayer all our concerns – personal, family, global, business, political, social – and open ourselves to what the Gospel has to say in each of these areas.

As I pray in this way, listening to the Lord's message in the gospels addressed to me personally in the whole of my real life situation, he will invite me to make real, practical decisions about how to live the Gospel. Because of the complexity of our lives today, it can be very necessary to seek some guidance in sifting what is truly significant in each one's Christian living. Members of various Christian churches are rediscovering the need and importance of spiritual direction for people committed to a life of prayer. As this need is being addressed, there is the growing possibility for each of us to find someone to help us in applying the Gospel to our lives and making truly effective decisions about living as a Christian today. Through this process the realities of our lives are progressively more united with the reality of the life of the risen Lord.

As we continue our contemplation of the gospels, right through the suffering and death of the Lord to his resurrection, our practical decisions about embracing discipleship are confirmed. We receive the strength to carry them out through the power communicated to us. Through this power we grow in the ability to live our whole lives in Christ risen, joyfully and productively for the coming of his kingdom.

Contemplating the Gospels

— 1 —
Contemplating the Trinity

'I will ask the Father, and he will give you another Advocate, to be with you forever. This is the Spirit of truth, whom the world cannot receive, because it neither sees him nor knows him. You know him, because he abides with you, and will be in you. Those who love me will keep my word, and my Father will love them, and we will come to them and make our home with them.'

John 14:15-17, 23

AS WE RETURN to 'ordinary time' after the contemplations of Lent and Easter, the church directs our attention, as the natural outcome of our Easter experience, to the great feasts of Pentecost and the Blessed Trinity. It is true to say that the mysteries of the coming of the Holy Spirit and of the Trinity are not well understood by many people. This is not because of any defect in their understanding, but rather due to the need to move away from the head to the level of the heart in considering these mysterious personal relationships.

Every day of our lives, we relate with many other persons. The way into such relationships is through our senses, especially seeing, hearing and touching. When we are separated from someone, we carry them with us in our memory and imagination through sensory 'images'. Our relationships acquire a permanence, and it is not difficult to keep them alive and active, even when we are absent from those people.

In the case of the Holy Spirit and the Trinity, the lack of immediate knowledge through the senses creates a problem for us. Some try to solve this problem by going straight to the head, the intellect. It is true that statements like, 'The Holy Spirit lives in me' or 'The Trinity is my life', can provide the subject matter of a really rich contemplation, commencing from our intellect. However, our humanness seems to demand an immediacy of personal contact, if not through the senses then at least through the imagination.

In his book of *The Spiritual Exercises*, St Ignatius of Loyola wanted to direct people to contemplate their personal relationship with the Trinity and the activity of the Trinity in the whole of Salvation History and in our world today. He left us the model of this contemplation in his exercise on the mystery of the Incarnation. Ignatius invites the contemplating person to join the Persons of the Trinity in their 'planning' of the Incarnation. In imagination we join the Trinity in seeing the whole world and all of its peoples in their struggles in need of redemption. We are present when the decree of Incarnation goes forth from Father, Son and Holy Spirit to the home of Mary in Nazareth of Galilee.

This may sound fanciful, 'just imagination'. True, it is our imagination that takes the place of our senses as the first point of personal contact, but there is far more involved here than just imagination. It expresses the profound, if mysterious, reality that the Trinity has made an eternal decree which is being fulfilled for the praying person as they pray here and now in time. In the words of Ignatius: 'Our Lord has just become man for me.'

The same truth about our immediate presence to the mystery applies to every gospel contemplation we make. Not only are we present to the Lord Jesus as he participates in the particular gospel setting, but we are present to the Trinity who accompany Jesus on every step of his journey, and to the same Trinity who are alive and active in our world at this moment.

If we wish to develop our relationship with the Holy Spirit or with the Persons of the Trinity, it is helpful to begin by recalling that it is primarily the Holy Spirit to whom God's dwelling within us is attributed. The gospel of John also makes it very clear that Jesus promises that he and the Father will also come to dwell in us. When we were baptized, we were baptized into the life (in the name) of Father, Son and Holy Spirit. It is the indwelling of the Holy Spirit that makes us children of God, and the Holy Spirit who cries out within us '*Abba*! Father!' (Romans 8:14-16).

While these theological reflections provide the background to our contemplation of the Spirit or of the Trinity, we may find that they do little to advance the all-important personal relationships. This is because our humanness requires the immediate presence that is provided by the senses, or by imagination, or by symbols.

It is alleged that St Patrick used the symbol of the shamrock to explain the mystery of the Trinity. If this is historically true, perhaps the shamrock evoked for Patrick a sense of personal relationship. Hopefully more than a solution to a mathematical riddle! Each of us must find our own personal symbols.

A great prayer symbol is the sign of the cross; or I may have a copy of my baptismal certificate to gaze at; or I may be helped by nature symbols like picking out three very similar trees or three outstanding stars (Orion's Belt, for example) and allowing them to represent for me Father, Son and Holy Spirit, so that as I contemplate each tree or each star I become more aware of my relationship with the particular Persons of the Trinity.

Whatever help to contemplation I have chosen, the essential truth remains that in contemplating the Persons of the Trinity I am getting in touch with the basic truth of my

Baptism and advancing my relationship with the Trinity which is my life. It would be most appropriate for me to conclude this contemplation with a time of conversation with each of the three Divine Persons.

— 2 —
Come, Lord Jesus

'Beware, keep alert; for you do not know when the time will come. It is like a man going on a journey, when he leaves home and puts his slaves in charge, each with his work, and commands the doorkeeper to be on the watch. Therefore keep awake; you do not know when the master of the house will come, in the evening, or at midnight, or at cockcrow or at dawn, or else he may find you asleep when he comes suddenly. And what I say to you I say to all: "Keep awake."'

Mark 13:33-37

THIS IS OUR GOSPEL READING for the first Sunday of Advent, Year B. We begin our prayer by focusing on the setting for the gospel text. Here it is the magnificent sight of the Temple of God in Jerusalem, in the last days of the life of Jesus before his suffering, death and resurrection. I allow my imagination to be captured by the person of Jesus, in whatever way he looks to me. I am immediately present to him who is always present to me by virtue of my baptism into Father, Son and Holy Spirit. I may rest for as long as I wish in contemplation of him. The text above, while leading us into contemplative presence to the Lord Jesus is also a wonderful challenge to us to engage in meditation on the great Christian truths it expounds.

Perhaps the first thing to notice about it, something perhaps surprising, is that it does not seem to look forward to the great, coming feast of Christmas, but rather recaptures the predominant theme of the readings for the end of the year which had been the constant theme of the previous week: the coming of the Lord at the end of time, and the sense of closure and finality that brings. The same theme is captured in the other readings for Years A and C from the gospels of Matthew (24:37-44) and Luke (21:25-28). This may well lead us to an awareness of the essential unity of the Christian mystery. Our ending is both our beginning and our looking forward in certain hope to what is to come.

The Lord Jesus is coming. Yes, he is coming this Christmas; he is coming into our world daily in great cosmic events, in small personal encounters; he is coming to me personally at the unknown moment of my death; he is coming in glory at 'the end of time'. Each and every one of these comings makes its demand on each and every person for awareness. What if he should come and I were to miss him!

The need to be aware, alert, on the watch, was a constant theme of the early church. Modern theologians often remark that the early Christians had a mistaken idea of the imminence of the Lord's Second Coming, evident in the writings of Paul and in the gospels. Or, could it be that the sacred writers had a true grasp of the fleetingness of human life compared to eternity!

The theme of watching (or being alert or awake) for the Lord's coming is evident in several parables, notably the one of the wise and the foolish bridesmaids (Matthew 25:1). It appears in the writings of Paul: 'Be persevering in your prayers, as you stay awake to pray' (Colossians 4:2), and of Peter: 'Be on the watch, because your enemy the devil is prowling round, like a roaring lion, looking for someone to devour' (1 Peter 5:8).

Not surprisingly, this theme is at the heart of one of the most important moments in the life of Jesus, his prayer in Gethsemane. Knowing the utter weakness of his disciples, and that they were about to lose faith, he warns them, 'Watch and pray that you do not come to the great trial.' The disciples, of course, fall asleep, no matter how many times Jesus warns them to stay awake. The only way they will learn to be awake, watchful and aware is through the redemption which is to come.

In the spirit of that same redemption we pray in the Lord's prayer: 'Save us from the time of trial.' Just as Jesus in Gethsemane urged his disciples in vain to stay awake, so in our brief reading above from Mark he exhorts us three times, in the beginning, in the middle and at the end: 'Stay awake!'

For all of the comings of the Lord – at each Christmas, for his daily comings into our lives, for the time of our personal death, for his 'coming in glory' – we pray. A favourite prayer of the early Christians was: '*Maranatha*. Come, Lord Jesus!' These are the concluding words in the Bible. They were prayed not to persuade the Lord to come, but in order that those praying would be awake, watchful, alert and aware and so not miss his coming.

In our liturgy, the priest prays after the Lord's Prayer, 'Deliver us, Lord, from every evil, and grant us your peace in our day. In your mercy keep us free from sin, and protect us from all anxiety, as we watch in joy and hope for the coming of our saviour, Jesus Christ.'

Certainly Jesus will come at the end of the life of each person to lead them home to the Father. But what of his coming into our lives at every moment of every day, those comings which we can easily miss unless we are aware and alert, in other words not sufficiently contemplative? It can be a great help at the end of each day to do an 'awareness examen' in which we look back and we remember, putting our day together in gratitude to the Lord for so many comings.

It is easy to recognize Jesus in the beauty of creation, in the warming sunshine, in the kindness of another person, but, as we grow in contemplation, we are also ready to recognize him in the difficulties and struggles of life, in suffering, in the poor, the lonely, even in those who challenge us by their apparent lack of kindness.

All is gift, and we receive every aspect of our day gratefully. We slowly learn with St Paul to give thanks to God in every circumstance, even in what we must struggle to accept.

— 3 —

Prayer Is Infallible

Jesus was praying in a certain place, and after he had finished one of his disciples said to him, 'Lord, teach us to pray, as John taught his disciples.' He said to them, 'When you pray, say:

> Father,
> Hallowed be your name.
> Your kingdom come.
> Give us each day our daily bread.
> And forgive us our sins,
>   for we ourselves forgive everyone who is indebted to us.
> And do not bring us to the time of trial.'

And he said to them, 'Suppose one of you has a friend, and you go to him at midnight and say to him, "Friend, lend me three loaves of bread; for a friend of mine has arrived, and I have nothing to set before him." And he answers from within, "Do not bother me; the door has already been locked, and my children are with me in bed; I cannot get up and give you anything." I tell you, even though he will not get up and give him anything because he is his friend, at least because of his persistence he will get up and give him whatever he needs.

'So I say to you, Ask and it will be given you; search, and you will find; knock, and the door will be opened for you. For everyone who asks receives, and everyone who searches finds, and for everyone who knocks the door will be opened. Is there anyone among you, if your child asks for bread, will give them a stone; or if your child asks for a fish, will give them a snake; or if your child asks for an egg, will give them a scorpion? If you then, who are evil, know how to give good gifts to your children, how much more will the heavenly Father give the Holy Spirit to those who ask him!'

Luke 11:1-13

THIS IS OUR GOSPEL READING for the Sunday of the 17th Week of Ordinary Time, Year C.

There is no doubting that of the four gospels Luke is quite outstanding in his portrait of Jesus as a praying person, and in his teaching about prayer. Luke mentions that Jesus was praying at all the key moments in his public life. It happens after his Baptism; it is while he is praying that the Holy Spirit descends upon him and he hears the Father's proclamation (3:21). Next, before naming the twelve apostles, he spends the whole night in prayer to God (6:12). Then, it was while he was praying alone that he asked his disciples, 'Who do you say that I am?' (9:18). It was while he was praying that the Transfiguration occurred (9:29). Finally, our present mystery happened at the end of a period of prayer. Each of the above five references to prayer is unique to the gospel of Luke. As we enter upon our contemplation, we may wish to spend some time gazing upon Jesus as he prays to the Father. In effect, by doing so we are united in prayer with him.

When the disciples ask for a lesson in prayer, Jesus gives them the Lord's Prayer. It is more original than the 'Our Father' of Matthew's chapter 6, simpler and briefer. Matthew's Lord's Prayer has been expanded for more rhythmical liturgical recitation. The words that appear only in Matthew are: 'our'; 'in heaven'; 'your will be done'; 'on earth as it is in heaven'; and 'but rescue us from the evil one'. Most people who pray Luke's

Lord's Prayer find that its simplicity is more intimate. Perhaps we can each profit by joining them, and seeing if we have a similar experience.

Jesus goes on to tell a parable about knocking on someone's door for bread in the middle of the night. It's understandable that the person in bed was reluctant to respond, but also understandable that if the friend kept on knocking, he'd get what he wanted. That, then, is the point of the parable. Parables usually have just one point. It is not legitimate to turn them into allegories, as, for instance, making the false comparison between the householder and God.

Luke continues, giving us a wonderful teaching from Jesus about the infallibility of prayer. Prayer is always answered. 'Ask, and it will be given to you.' The lesson is plain and clear; however, Jesus goes on to say it five more times. Prayer must be infallible!

The lesson is further driven home by appealing to the relationship between a loving parent and their child. What parent could possibly give a stone instead of bread, a snake instead of a fish, or a scorpion instead of an egg? The conclusion is starkly obvious, and, if that wasn't enough, we are left to contemplate how much the infinitely loving Father excels in generosity the most loving of parents. That is the force of the remark: '... you who are evil'. It is not a statement of wickedness apart from its context. It is simply the comparison of our fallible human love with infinite divine love. 'How much more will the heavenly Father give the Holy Spirit to those who ask him!' In the corresponding place Matthew writes (7:11): '... how much more will your Father in heaven give good things to those who ask him!'

Luke's naming the Holy Spirit arises not just from his being the one gospel which most emphasizes the role of the Holy Spirit, but it points to a very important lesson in the infallibility of prayer. It is absolutely appropriate that we should begin any prayer with attention to the human concerns uppermost in our minds. God welcomes our prayer for a dying friend. God also welcomes our prayer to win the lottery. The latter is at least an acknowledgment of God's generosity and sovereignty over the whole of reality.

Prayer is a two-way relationship. God always gives the Holy Spirit – without fail. It is futile to complain, 'I don't want the Holy Spirit; I want the winning lottery ticket.' Such a complaint would show a total misunderstanding of what prayer is.

No matter what the starting-point is for any particular prayer, it is of the essence that the praying person is open to change, growth and development in their relationship with God. In the two greatest prayers of petition in scripture – that of Jesus in Gethsemane and Paul's prayer to be delivered from 'the thorn in the flesh' – neither Jesus nor Paul received what they started out asking for, but both were answered and grew in relationship with the Holy Spirit.

— 4 —
Bartimaeus

They came to Jericho. As he and his disciples and a large crowd were leaving Jericho, Bartimaeus, son of Timaeus, a blind beggar, was sitting by the roadside. When he heard that it was Jesus of Nazareth, he began to shout out and say, 'Jesus, Son of David, have mercy on me!' Many ordered him to be quiet, but he cried out even more loudly, 'Son of David, have mercy on me!' Jesus stood still and said, 'Call him here.' And they called the blind man, saying to him, 'Take heart; get up, he's calling you.' So, throwing off his cloak, he sprang up and came to Jesus. Then Jesus said to him, 'What do you want me to do for you?' The blind man said to him, 'My teacher, let me see again. Jesus said to him, 'Go; your faith has made you well.' Immediately he regained his sight and followed him in the way.

Mark 10:46-52

THE GOSPEL OF THE HEALING of Bartimaeus is read on the 30th Sunday of the year (B) and Thursday of the 8th week of Ordinary Time.

The theme of light and darkness plays a big part in the gospels, especially the gospel of John. Already in his great prologue John announces that there was a light shining in the darkness, and the darkness could not overcome it. John the Baptist was a witness to the light and the true light (Jesus) which enlightens everyone was coming into the world (John 1:5-9). When Jesus does come, he proclaims: 'I am the light of the world. Whoever follows me will never walk in darkness, but will have the light of life' (John 8:12).

This is the prelude to the great drama of the healing of the man who had been blind from birth (John, chapter 9). Healing of blindness is a feature of the synoptics also. Jesus had already announced in Luke (4:18) that part of his mission was to proclaim new sight for the blind. Both Matthew and Luke repeat our story of the healing of Bartimaeus, without naming him. Matthew, in fact, turns him into two blind men, as he does with the Gerasene demoniac. In his Jewishness, Matthew sees salvation as coming to groups rather than individuals. He even has two donkeys in the story of the procession of palms!

The healing of Bartimaeus has a very significant position in the gospel of Mark. It appears at the end of the tenth chapter, after the healing at Bethsaida of another blind man (the one who saw people who looked like trees walking) in the eighth chapter. This is the literary convention of inclusion, in which what appears at the beginning and the end of a piece of writing names an important theme of what comes in between.

What does come between? The threefold prophecy by Jesus of his coming suffering, death and resurrection, and the requirement for disciples to follow him in that way, which the disciples in their blindness do not begin to grasp. Each time Jesus makes the prophecy, they are having an argument about the exact opposite – who among them will be the greatest in the kingdom?

So we come to contemplate Bartimaeus and his healing. What an engaging character he is! And what a fine picture Mark paints of the interaction between him and Jesus. Mark is famous for including in his stories what read like true eyewitness details, and we are certainly not short of them in this mystery. We begin, as always, by recalling our baptism, our presence to the persons of the Trinity who are always present to us. They are always present to Jesus as the mystery unfolds, and also to us as we contemplate. We offer to the Trinity our time of prayer, that all of our intentions, actions and inner operations may be directed to the glory of God and the coming of the kingdom.

We enter upon our contemplation by composing ourselves for prayer, taking a posture with a straight back, alert but relaxed. Attention to slow, deep breathing certainly helps towards this. Then we allow ourselves to picture the scene closer to the famous walls of Jericho. We see Jesus, the disciples, the crowd of people, and our blind beggar Bartimaeus seated by the roadside, wearing his cloak and rattling his tin.

We can pause for a while to see what each of these persons looks like in our imagination. We then pray for the grace we are seeking: first, to know Jesus more intimately, to love him more ardently, and to follow him with growing commitment. We add to this prayer one for whatever grace we are now personally seeking.

We are already present to the disciples of Jesus and to a large crowd. Now they fade as Jesus and Bartimaeus take centre stage. How does Mark present Bartimaeus? As an uninhibited extrovert – after all, he has nothing to lose. So he shouts out. What does he shout? 'Jesus son of David, have mercy on me.' This is a key moment in the history of Christian prayer. The prayer of Bartimaeus became the formula used in the Eastern churches of the early centuries as the 'Jesus Prayer'. Its endless repetition opened the way of contemplation and mysticism to generations of saints in those churches, both canonized and not. A frequent way of using the prayer was to begin with the words as quoted by Mark, and gradually to simplify it until all the contemplative did was to repeat the name 'Jesus' over and over – a sure way of simply being in his presence in deep prayer of the heart.

The crowd now come back into the action. They were

tagging along behind Jesus 'the important man,' so they sternly told the insignificant beggar to be quiet. Jesus stood still. Let me be still too, and contemplate Jesus as he says, 'Call him here.' Perhaps he wants me to come to him; or perhaps he wants me to invite someone in need to come into his presence.

At least some members of the crowd really hear this word of Jesus, and undergo a conversion. The tone of their address to Bartimaeus is now so sympathetic – 'Take heart; get up, he is calling you.' Bartimaeus needs no urging. Still the typical extrovert, he throws off his cloak (to begin running), and comes to Jesus. Jesus humorously but sincerely asks, 'What do you want me to do for you?' The answer is obvious – 'My teacher, let me see again.' 'Go; your faith (your personal relationship with me) has made you well.'

When he regained his sight, Bartimaeus followed Jesus in the way. At the start of our story, Bartimaeus was beside the road, now he is in the way. Both times Mark wrote the same Greek word, meaning 'way'. To be in the way is to be in union with Jesus, who declares himself to be the Way (John 14:6). What a happy ending for our friend Bartimaeus!

I may find myself wanting to enter into dialogue with him, with Jesus, or with other persons involved in this mystery. Or I may wish to pray to Mary and to the Persons of the Trinity for the grace I am now seeking.

— 5 —

In His Right Mind

The following reading is the gospel for the Monday of the 4th Week of Ordinary Time. It is quite a bit longer than our usual readings in this series. However, the text itself is such a beautifully wrought complete unit that it deserves to be quoted in full. It also provides ample material for *Lectio Divina*, so is scarcely in need of much commentary.

> They came to the other side of the sea, to the country of the Gerasenes. And when he had stepped out of the boat, immediately a man out of the tombs, with an unclean spirit, met him. He lived among the tombs, and no one could restrain him any more, even with a chain; for he had often been restrained with shackles and chains, but the chains he wrenched apart, and the shackles he broke in pieces; and no one had the strength to subdue him. Night and day among the tombs he was always howling and bruising himself with stones.
>
> When he saw Jesus from a distance he ran and bowed down before him; and he shouted at the top of his voice, 'What have you to do with me, Jesus, Son of the Most High God? I adjure you, by God, do not torment me.' For he had said to him, 'Come out of the man, you unclean spirit!' Then Jesus asked him, 'What is your name?' He replied, 'My name is Legion, for we are many.' He begged him earnestly not to send them out of the country.
>
> Now there on the hillside a great herd of swine was feeding, and the unclean spirits begged him, 'Send us into the swine; let us enter them.' So he gave them permission.

And the unclean spirits came out and entered the swine; and the herd, numbering about two thousand, rushed down the steep bank into the sea, and were drowned in the sea.

The swineherds ran off and told it in the city and in the country. Then people came to see what it was that had happened. They came to Jesus and saw the demoniac sitting there, clothed and in his right mind, the very man who had had the legion; and they were afraid. Those who had seen what had happened to the demoniac and to the swine reported it. Then they began to beg Jesus to leave their neighbourhood.

As he was getting into the boat, the man who had been possessed by demons begged him that he might be with him. But Jesus refused, and said to him, 'Go home to your friends, and tell them how much the Lord has done for you, and what mercy he has shown you.' And he went away and began to proclaim in the Decapolis how much Jesus had done for him; and everyone was amazed.

Mark 5:1-20

Mark's gospel is the one most concerned with demonic possession. In all he treats of the subject five times. Matthew and Luke each repeat some of these events, but add no new ones of their own. It seems to be a pattern with those 'possessed' that the demons in them attempt to confront Jesus by claiming knowledge about his identity. In the first of the exorcisms (Mark 1:23-27, very early indeed in Mark's gospel), the evil spirits exclaim, 'What have you to do with us, Jesus of Nazareth? Have you come to destroy us? I know who you are, the Holy One of God.' This is typical of the Jewish philosophy that to name someone is to assert some sort of power over them.

The typical response of Jesus is to impose silence on the evil spirit. The second reference to exorcism comes very soon after the first. 'He cured many who were sick with various diseases, and cast out many demons, and he would not permit the demons to speak because they knew him' (Mark 1:34). Here we have the clear link between illness and demonic possession, common in the thinking at the time of Jesus.

The failure to be aware of this link gave rise to the hitherto almost universal opinion that Mary of Magdala was a great sinner (which was thought to mean a prostitute, as if this was the only sin open to women!). When Luke mentions the women who were disciples of Jesus in his mission (Luke 8:2-3), he names Mary Magdalene, 'from whom seven devils had gone out'. This may mean no more than that she was cured of severe illness. The fifth of Mark's stories of demonic possession, that of the boy whose father brought him to the disciples of Jesus for healing (Mark 9:14-29), is clearly recognized by modern scholars as a case of epilepsy.

So we come to the greatest exorcism story, that of the Gerasene demoniac. What was the initial state of this unfortunate man when he met Jesus? His whole existence was in a mess. He was cut off from all human relationships. He lived alone, among the tombs, signifying a morbid fascination with death. Incapable of any authentic life, he associates himself with the dead. He has lost all sense of identity. The demons are named 'legion' because he no longer has a unified personality. He is no longer capable of personal relationship. He displays classical signs of profound psychological disturbance.

As is common in such cases, he is more like a wild animal than a human being; he was howling and self-mutilating; he runs about naked (clearly implied in Mark's remark that, after his healing, he was clothed). He displays that strange psychological phenomenon of superhuman strength, able to break chains and shackles. After his encounter with Jesus and the exorcism, not only is he clothed but 'in his right mind'. It is as if he has become human again. Surely this ranks among the greatest healing stories of the gospels.

Jesus came into this world to combat evil in all its forms – spiritual, psychological and physical, global and personal. Nothing is too great for him to overcome. Mark tells the story of this exorcism very briefly and simply. Jesus exercises divine power: 'Come out of the man, you unclean spirit.'

The healing is immediate and total. Is it possible for a healing so radical to take place instantaneously? Yes – examples of such cures from extreme psychological conditions are well attested. This does not, of course, imply that we can bypass the often long and difficult process of human rehabilitation.

The man who had been possessed now becomes fully human, 'clothed and in his right mind'. He is able to enter again into relationship. Jesus tells him to go home. What a deep meaning that word now has for him. He is to share the good news with his own people, as an active apostle telling his friends what mercy the Lord has shown him.

The gospels repeatedly contrast the loving, saving actions of Jesus with the crass, narrow-minded attitudes of the crowds. Here 'they were afraid', because the man was now liberated from the stereotype into which they had fitted him for a long time.

There remains the peripheral question about the pigs and their deprived owner! Did Jesus act justly in his regard? It is not a real issue. Perhaps we should regard this detail of the story as non-historical. What Mark is teaching is the gospel value of the human person. All other considerations are secondary. In the sight of God the value of a single human person is paramount. Thank God in our own day we have repeated examples of this, in which heroic persons disregard expense, risk and self-sacrifice to save the lives of others.

I may be drawn to converse with the now fully healed 'Gerasene demoniac', with his friends and relations, with the crowds, or with Jesus himself, and the Divine Persons.

—6—
Storm at Sea

On that day, when evening had come, Jesus said to them, 'Let us go across to the other side.' And, leaving the crowd behind, they took him with them in the boat, just as he was. Other boats were with him. A great windstorm arose, and the waves beat into the boat, so that the boat was already being swamped. But he was in the stern, asleep on the cushion; and they woke him up and said to him, 'Teacher, do you not care that we are perishing?' He woke up and rebuked the wind, and said to the sea, 'Peace! Be still!' Then the wind ceased, and there was a dead calm. He said to them, 'Why are you afraid? Have you still no faith?' And they were filled with great awe and said to one another, 'Who then is this, that even the wind and the sea obey him?'

Mark 4:35-41

THIS IS THE GOSPEL READING for the 12th Sunday of Ordinary Time, Year B, and for Saturday of the 3rd week of the year.

Early in the gospels of Mark and Luke, and fairly early in Matthew, we have this story of the first of the 'nature miracles' of Jesus, the calming of the storm on the sea of Galilee.

I prepare myself for the contemplation of this mystery of the Lord by slowly and thoughtfully approaching the place I have chosen for prayer. I stop a few paces away, and, standing upright, back straight, I spend a few moments breathing deeply, being attentive and aware of the air as it enters and leaves my lungs. I then say a formal prayer to offer to God this time of contemplation: 'Lord, I ask for the grace that all that I am and all I do may be directed purely to your service and praise.'

I now move to the position for my prayer. Before my imagination has time to wander, I see in imagination the scene where these events occur: the sea of Galilee, about 16 kilometres in length from north to south, about 12 kilometres in breadth from east to west, nestling in its basin among surrounding hills. Its location keeps it usually calm, but when the wind springs up, it can be subject to violent storms. I begin to pray for the grace I seek: always, as I come to the gospel, I ask to grow in personal knowledge of Jesus, to love him more fully and follow him more closely. In this context there may also be a prayer for some practical aspect of that following in my life that I am seeking.

I become aware of the Persons involved with me in this contemplation. I always attend to the presence of Father, Son and Holy Spirit into whom I have been baptized. Each was present to Jesus and his disciples as he lived out this mystery of a real, life-threatening storm on the lake. Each is present to me as I live out my unique mission for the coming of the kingdom in the world of today. Perhaps I want to give expression to my relationship with the Father, the Son or the Holy Spirit. Am I ready to converse with any of the Divine Persons?

As I am ready, I move into the material of this particular contemplation. I slowly read over Mark's account of it a couple of times. Of all four gospels, Mark is the one who reads most like an eyewitness account in the small detail he gives. Here he is the only one who mentions that it was evening. Also that the disciples took him aboard (after all, it was their boat!). Not only that, they took him 'just as he was'. How was he? He was tired after teaching the very large crowd that had gathered on the shore of the lake in Mark 4:1. He was in his ordinary clothes, not weatherproof, sea-going gear. 'Other boats were with him.' I wonder how they weathered the storm: at least they benefited from the calming of it by Jesus.

Tired out, Jesus fell asleep: only in Mark, 'in the stern of the boat, with his head on the cushion.' Perhaps before the storm hits, I have the chance to be present to the persons involved, to Jesus, as he sleeps, to the twelve apostles who have just been named and appointed in the previous chapter (Mark 3:13-19). I may want to speak with one or other, and ask for their intercession. All authentic prayer involves personal relationship: here, not only with Jesus, but with anyone in the action, as well as with the Persons of the Trinity.

Following the structure recommended by Ignatius, I may move on to hear what they say and see what they do. The dialogue between the disciples is much more confrontational in Mark than in the other two. This fits in with the whole tone of their relationship throughout the gospel.

Mark stresses the point that the disciples of Jesus continually misunderstand him, because their thoughts are 'not on divine things, but on human things' (8:33). They are not contemplative enough to understand a suffering and serving Messiah. Here Matthew writes that they said, 'Lord, save us; we are perishing.' In Luke they shout, 'Master, Master, we are perishing.' In Mark, accusingly, 'Teacher, do you not care that we are perishing?'

Then we have the only real action, but what an action it was: Jesus woke up, rebuked the wind, and said to the sea, 'Peace! Be still!' And there was a dead calm. As I pray, am I moved to open up to the risen Lord any storm I may be involved with in my life, and allow Jesus to take charge of it?

In the calm that follows the storm Jesus speaks. In Luke he simply asks them to look into their hearts: 'Where is your faith?' In Matthew, 'Why are you afraid, you of little faith?' In Mark,

Jesus rebukes his disciples, 'Why are you afraid? Have you still no faith?' Confrontational, but a real relationship. What do I want to say to Jesus? Or to any of the disciples? Or to Mary? Or to Father, Son or Holy Spirit?

I conclude my conversations with a formal prayer – to Mary, the Hail Mary, to Jesus the *Anima Christi*, to the Father, to whom I pray in the Holy Spirit with the Son the Lord's Prayer from Luke, slowly and reflectively:

> Father, hallowed be your name;
> Your kingdom come.
> Give us each day our daily bread.
> Forgive us our sins; for we ourselves
> forgive those who are indebted to us.
> And do not bring us to the time of trial.

— 7 —
Lazarus

Now a certain man was ill, Lazarus of Bethany, from the village of Mary and her sister Martha. Mary was the one who anointed the Lord with perfume and wiped his feet with her hair; her brother Lazarus was ill. So the sisters sent a message to Jesus, 'Lord, he whom you love is ill.' But, when Jesus heard it, he said, 'This illness does not lead to death; rather it is for God's glory so that the Son of Man may be glorified through it.' Accordingly, even though Jesus loved Martha, and her sister, and Lazarus, after he heard that Lazarus was ill, he stayed two days longer in the place where he was.

Then after this, he said to his disciples, 'Let us go to Judea again.' The disciples said to him, 'Rabbi, the Jews were just now trying to stone you, and are you going there again?' Jesus answered, 'Our friend Lazarus has fallen asleep, but I am going to awaken him.' The disciples said to him, 'Lord, if he has fallen asleep, he will be all right.' Jesus, however, had been speaking about his death, but they thought that he was referring merely to sleep. Then he told them plainly, 'Lazarus is dead. For your sake I am glad I was not there, so that you may believe. But let us go to him.' Thomas, who was called the Twin, said to his fellow disciples, 'Let us go also that we may die with him.'

When Jesus arrived, he found that Lazarus had already been in the tomb four days. Martha said to Jesus, 'Lord, if you had been here, my brother would not have died. But even now I know that God will give you whatever you ask of him.' Jesus said to her, 'Your brother will rise again.' Martha said to him, 'I know that he will rise again at the resurrection of the last day.' Jesus said to her, 'I am the resurrection and the life. Those who believe in me, even though they die, will live, and everyone who lives and believes in me will never die. Do you believe this?' She said to him, 'Yes, Lord, I believe that you are the Messiah, the Son of God, the one coming into the world.'

When Mary came to where Jesus was and saw him, she knelt at his feet and said to him, 'Lord, if you had been here, my brother would not have died.' When Jesus saw her weeping, and the Jews who came with her also weeping, he was greatly disturbed in spirit and deeply moved. He said, 'Where have you laid him?' They said to him, 'Come and see.' So the Jews said, 'See how he loved him.'

Then Jesus, again greatly disturbed, came to the tomb. It was a cave, and a stone was lying against it. Jesus said, 'Take away the stone.' Martha said to him, 'Lord, already there is a stench because he has been dead four days.' Jesus said to her, 'Did I not tell you that, if you believed, you would see the glory of God?' So they took away the stone. And Jesus looked upward and said, 'Father, I thank you for having heard me. I know that you always hear me, but I have said this for the sake of the crowd standing here, so that they believe that you sent me.'

When he had said this, he cried out with a loud voice, 'Lazarus, come out!' The dead man came out, his hands and feet bound with strips of cloth, and his face wrapped in a cloth. Jesus said, 'Unbind him, and let him go.'

John 11:1-44 (abridged)

Lazarus

THIS IS THE GOSPEL of the 5th Sunday of Lent, Year A. It is presented here in slightly abridged form, omitting mainly the section about Mary staying in the house.

After my usual steps of recollecting myself, coming to peaceful awareness, perhaps through attending to my breathing, or to the sounds around me, I see in imagination the setting for this contemplation: the village of Bethany on the mount of Olives, only a couple of kilometres to the east of Jerusalem. I come to this mystery of the Lord, aware that it is a momentous one of great solemnity and power. Jesus is presented to us as putting his own life in immediate danger for one whom he loves. He has done this for me too, so I ask to know him, love him and follow him. He wants me to have 'life in abundance' (John 10:10); so I pray that I may be open to receive whatever gift of healing he wants me to have now.

The four gospels contain many stories of the exercise by Jesus of his mission of healing. In so far as I suffer hurt, guilt, fear, grief, anxiety, resentment or rejection, I am in need of the Lord's healing power and touch. Different gospel stories of personal healing reveal to us attitudes we need if through our prayer we are to meet the Lord in his role as Healer. The first essential is that we be open to revealing our need for healing to another person. This puts my wound 'out there' in the real world, the world of God's love, rather than 'in here' festering within my unhealed mind. Second, I must be open to the possibility of receiving professional help from a counsellor or other therapist, should that be needed.

If I am to allow the Lord to heal me in contemplative prayer, it will be through the exercise of my faith in him. I need to trust him like the leper who said without a moment's doubt, 'If you want to, you can heal me' (Mark 1:40). Another lesson the gospels teach through the story of the paralytic beside the pool in John, chapter 5, is that 'time is not the enemy'. For him it was a matter of 38 years; then he met Jesus in his healing mission. This story has another important teaching for us. We must really want to be healed. How often do we simply hang on to our hurts through force of habit. Jesus asked him, 'Do you want to be healed?' (John 5:6). I must really want it.

Whatever about the historicity of Jesus raising the dead, the story of Lazarus has profound fruit for anyone entering it in contemplation. It is a climax in John's account of the ministry of Jesus. Jesus puts his own life on the line by returning to Jerusalem where he knows well the risk involved. He is willing to lose his life to give his friend new life, exactly what he will accomplish through his death-resurrection.

The text of the story is full of power, whether we choose to make our contemplation through *Lectio Divina* or through entering in imagination into relationship with the persons, seeing who they are for us, hearing what they are saying, seeing what they are doing. We then reflect upon our own real life situation and enter into conversation in whatever way we are drawn: perhaps with Jesus, perhaps with his mother, Mary, perhaps asking them to lead us into speaking with the persons of the Trinity, perhaps with any of the characters in this great drama.

The sisters send a message to Jesus: 'Lord, the one whom you love is ill.' I know who that means; it is me. The reply of Jesus is relevant to my situation, 'This sickness will not lead to death; rather it is for God's glory.' Here faith is put to a reality test. Do I believe that the Lord can heal me? Do I believe he wants to? Do I believe I will receive the grace to let him?

So often in matters of healing, Scripture mentions a delay of a couple of days to go through the healing process. It even applies to the resurrection of Jesus! Here, Jesus delays for two days before setting out for Bethany. When he does take the road, good old brash Thomas says, 'Let's go, so we can die with him.' Brave words, which will have to wait quite a while for their fulfilment. We see the two sisters, so consistent in personality with other portraits of them: Martha, the practical, outgoing extrovert, Mary the more introvert contemplative one who remains in the house while Martha is out on the road to meet Jesus. Where am I?

As the time for the great happening approaches, Jesus enters into dialogue with each of the sisters. They both start by saying to him, 'Lord, if you had been here, my brother would not have died.'

With Martha there is more of an intellectual discussion about resurrection, which leads Jesus to the profound reply, 'I am the resurrection and the life. Those who believe into me, even though they die, will live, and everyone who lives and believes into me will never die.' The discussion ends with Martha's making a very formal theological pronouncement, 'Yes, Lord, I believe that you are the Messiah, the Son of God, the one coming into the world.' The testing of her faith will come shortly.

With Mary, the less intellectual and less work-driven, her reaction is one of weeping. Jesus responds to her by joining her in weeping, as well as by being 'greatly disturbed in spirit and deeply moved'.

When they go to the tomb, John mentions a second time that Jesus was greatly disturbed. The reason seems to be that Jesus was not choosing to act like one in complete control who knew exactly what he was going to do. Rather he truly humanly experienced grief in union with the grief of Mary and Martha.

When he asked for the removal of the stone, Martha's former profession of faith fell short. She objected, 'Lord, already there is a stench, because he has been dead four days.' What of my faith? Am I willing really to believe that the risen Lord can bring alive in me parts that I have allowed to die? Do I safely put my faith to one side in a neat little theological compartment, or am I willing to be open to a real, personal relationship with Jesus who wants to heal me? Can he really heal me? Or do I think it is too late, as Martha did?

When Jesus spoke, the dead man came out of his tomb. Am I willing to leave my tomb, and to hear the word of Jesus, 'Unbind him, and let him go.' Who is with me now in my prayer to help unbind me?

As I am moved, I re-enter conversation with any of the persons involved in this mystery, or with Mary, or the Father, the Son or the Holy Spirit.

— 8 —

Lenten Conversion

Jesus said, 'Beware of practising your piety before others in order to be seen by them; for then you have no reward from your Father in heaven.

'So, whenever you give alms, do not sound a trumpet before you, as the hypocrites do in the synagogues and in the streets, so that they may be praised by others. Truly I tell you, they have received their reward. But when you give alms, do not let your left hand know what your right hand is doing, so that your alms may be done in secret; and your Father who sees in secret will reward you.

'And whenever you pray, do not be like the hypocrites; for they love to stand and pray in the synagogues and at the street corners, so that they may be seen by others. Truly I tell you, they have received their reward. But whenever you pray, go into your room and shut the door and pray to your Father who is in secret; and your Father who sees in secret will reward you.

And whenever you fast do not look dismal, like the hypocrites, for they disfigure their faces so as to show others they are fasting. Truly I tell you, they have received their reward. But when you fast, put oil on your head and wash your face, so that your fasting may be seen not by others but by your Father who is in secret; and your Father who sees in secret will reward you.'

Matthew 6:1-6, 16-18

THIS IS THE GOSPEL READING each year for Ash Wednesday.

As I begin to pray with this passage, I start, as always, by recalling God's presence to me and my deep desire to be present to the Lord in this time of prayer. I offer to him the time which I have allotted for this contemplation. I recall the grace of my baptism, union with Father, Son and Holy Spirit, and my trust that through this prayer that union will grow and deepen.

The text chosen by the church for this Ash Wednesday gospel is from the basic Christian message of the Sermon on the Mount. I am about to meditate on the words of Matthew attributed to Jesus. I must remember that these are not simply historical in our modern understanding of that term but are Matthew's profound and beautifully crafted reflection on the tradition of what Jesus said during his life on earth.

I commence by recalling the setting given by Matthew in his gospel. A crowd of people had gathered on a hilltop to hear the words of Jesus, the greatest of the prophets. Prominent among the crowd are the chosen disciples of Jesus. I may find myself present as a disciple, as I truly am by my baptism, or present simply as a member of the crowd. What is important is that I am truly present to him who is my Life. I contemplate not just the spoken words, but the person of the speaker.

The passage chosen for Ash Wednesday has a clear and cogent structure in its treatment of the three spiritual activities recommended: almsgiving, prayer and fasting. Each is to be done in secret in the presence of God, who will reward us.

We must be careful not to overstress the idea of reward. Matthew, the most Jewish of the four gospels, writes repeatedly about reward and punishment because these ideas loomed so large in the minds of his Jewish readers. We must avoid carrying this over into an idea of bargaining with God, or, even worse, of achieving salvation through our own efforts.

One of the most important aspects of our passage is the order in which Jesus announces the three recommended activities of almsgiving, prayer and fasting. Matthew makes it clear in his great parable of the Last Judgment in chapter 25 that the sole criterion for God's judgment of us will be our practical charity to the poor, the stranger, the sick and the imprisoned.

It is not surprising then that the first and most important aspect of our Lenten observance is a renewal of this kind of practical love, summed up in the word 'almsgiving'. The exercise of monetary generosity is important. But we could well challenge ourselves in this Lent to the further and far more significant step of becoming personally involved in helping someone in need. None of us has to look far to find someone in need of our special love!

There has been a definite shift in the mentality of Christians in this regard since the second Vatican Council. In pre-conciliar days, the prime emphasis was on the individual's personal purification, to be achieved through the third of our trilogy, fasting, and this was to be taken in the most literal sense of that word. Now, as in our gospel text, the prime place belongs, as it does in the words of Jesus, to simple, sincere, authentic love.

The second of the three spiritual activities recommended for our Lenten observance is the renewal of our prayer life. Once again this is something that has undergone a revolution in the renewal called for by Vatican II. The church has moved from urging its members to recite vocal prayers to encouraging them to practise a variety of different authentic styles of prayer. Among them there is surely something for each individual in their endeavours to find their own unique way of relating to God. Even if I feel well set in my personal way of praying, I could profit by trying some other way with the hope of enriching my life of prayer.

Third, there is the question of self-discipline, summed up in the word 'fasting'. Many can recall a time when our approach to Lent was dominated by giving up something pleasant in order to achieve a further level of self-control. Many a Christian seemed to be more influenced by ancient Greek Stoicism than by the Gospel! Yet, perhaps more than ever, there is a need for discipline to move towards more healthy ways of eating and drinking!

Lent is a truly great season because it focuses on the primary challenge of the Gospel, the challenge to conversion of heart. 'Repent and believe the Good News' (Mark 1:15). Conversion is a sheer gift of God's grace, never attainable through our own efforts, but we can best prepare to receive that gift by observing the great trilogy of Jesus: 'almsgiving, prayer and fasting'.

— 9 —
A Woman's Conversion

One of the Pharisees asked Jesus to eat with him, and he went into the Pharisee's house and took his place at table. And a woman in the city who was a sinner, having learned that he was eating at the Pharisee's house, brought an alabaster jar of ointment. She stood behind him at his feet weeping, and began to bathe his feet with her tears and to dry them with her hair. Then she continued kissing his feet and anointing them with the ointment.

Now when the Pharisee who had invited him saw it, he said to himself, 'If this man were a prophet, he would have known who and what kind of woman this is who is touching him – that she is a sinner.' Jesus spoke up and said to him, 'Simon, I have something to say to you.' 'Teacher', he replied, 'speak.'

'A certain creditor had two debtors; one owed him five hundred denarii, and the other fifty. When they could not pay, he cancelled the debts for both of them. Now which of them will love him more?' Simon answered, 'I suppose the one for whom he cancelled the greater debt.' And Jesus said to him, 'You have judged rightly.'

Then, turning to the woman, he said to Simon, 'Do you see this woman? I entered your house; you gave me no water for my feet, but she has bathed my feet with her tears and dried them with her hair. You gave me no kiss, but from the time I came in she has not stopped kissing my feet. You did not anoint my head with oil, but she has anointed my feet with ointment. Therefore, I tell you, her sins, which were many, have been forgiven; hence she has shown great love. But the one to whom little is forgiven loves little.'

Then he said to her 'Your sins are forgiven.' But those who were at table with him began to say among themselves, 'Who is this who even forgives sins?' And he said to the woman, 'Your faith has saved you; go in peace.'

Luke 7:36-50

THIS IS THE GOSPEL for the 7th Sunday, Year C. It is clearly one of the most beautifully crafted stories of Luke, the great story teller. As such it lends itself to the style of contemplation so dear to St Ignatius in his *Spiritual Exercises*.

As Ignatius did in the contemplation of the Lord's Incarnation, we may well begin by situating ourselves with the Trinity as they gaze upon Jesus living out this mystery in his mission of universal love and compassion. Father, Son and Holy Spirit are present to all persons on the face of the earth in their desperate need for salvation.

As I join them in this presence, do I experience a call to be more like Jesus in bringing love and compassion to all I meet? If I find myself wanting to stay with these considerations in the presence of the three Divine Persons, I may linger as long as I like, and postpone going to Simon's dinner party to a later time of prayer.

When I do get to the house of Simon, I take in the scene in whatever way my imagination leads me. As a Pharisee, Simon is probably far from being poor. Perhaps I notice that the house has columns and is open and airy. I see the long tables for the reclining guests, perhaps the jars and basins for the customary washings. Each person makes up their own composition before entering on the matter for contemplation. I ask for the grace I want: always in gospel contemplation to know, love and follow

A Woman's Conversion

Jesus more intimately. There may be some specific grace I am drawn to pray for at this time.

I enter on my contemplation by entering once again into the scene, now fixing my gaze on the persons involved. Surely I must first become aware of Jesus. He is a young man, in the prime of life, very attractive to look upon. But the woman who comes into the room sees more deeply than that. No doubt aware of what he has meant to so many people in his public ministry, she senses in him a hope to be relieved of the burden of her up till now life of sin.

As I look, what do I sense in him, aware as I am of the full story of who he is? I see the unnamed woman as Luke presents her: silent (in the whole story she never speaks), but progressively becoming more active. I see Simon the Pharisee, looking perplexed at what happens as the events unfold. Then the other guests. What do they make of it all? I allow myself to be drawn into the scene, and into relationship with one or more of these persons.

People who do this contemplation almost universally report that they are drawn into the scene by conversing with one or other of the participants, and even 'becoming' one of them. Do I find myself identifying with Jesus? What do I say to him, and he to me? Perhaps I identify with the woman. I may ask her how she feels as the action unfolds. How do I feel? What do I say to her and she to me? Am I really like Simon, so that I begin to identify with him? Am I one of the bystanders? What do I make of it all from this perspective? Can I simply allow myself to be led by the Holy Spirit into whatever is going on deep within me?

As always in my contemplation or *Lectio Divina* I stop and remain quiet wherever I find fruit for my prayer life.

I see what each of the persons does: Jesus, totally aware of what is going on in the woman, in Simon, in the other guests, in me, remaining still and quiet, allowing the action to unfold, until the time comes for him to speak.

I listen carefully to what each person says: in their words as quoted by Luke, or deep within themselves, in their silence.

I reflect upon myself. What does Jesus now offer me? Could it be a deeper forgiveness for my worst sin, enabling me really to forgive myself, to rejoice in the Lord's forgiving love and to know myself as a totally forgiven sinner, who is now really free?

I don't forget to speak to Mary, to Jesus, to the other persons present and to the Father, Son and Holy Spirit, in whose presence the reality of this mystery of the Lord unfolds and who are now present to me as I pray.

— 10 —

God, Be Merciful

Jesus told this parable to some who trusted in themselves that they were righteous and treated others with contempt: 'Two men went up to the Temple to pray, one a Pharisee and the other a tax collector. The Pharisee, standing by himself, was praying thus, "God, I thank you that I am not like other people: thieves, rogues, adulterers, or even like this tax collector. I fast twice a week; I give a tenth of my income."

'But the tax collector, standing far off, would not even look up to heaven, but was beating his breast and saying, "God, be merciful to me a sinner!" I tell you, this man went down to his home justified rather than the other; for all who exalt themselves will be humbled, but all who humble themselves will be exalted.'

Luke 18:9-14

THIS IS THE GOSPEL for Saturday of the 3rd Week of Lent, and for Sunday of the 30th Week of Ordinary Time, Year C.

From Luke, the evangelist who far more than any of the other three focuses on the Lord's mercy, we have this very short, but beautifully constructed parable of forgiveness. It is indeed a lesson for us in contemplation.

We go through our usual process before entering upon this time of contemplation. We pause to collect ourselves a few paces away from the place in which we are going to pray. We take a few deep breaths, and slowly move to making our preparatory prayer of offering this time of contemplation, together with all our intentions, actions and interior operations, for the greater glory of God and the coming of God's kingdom.

The setting for our prayer is the Temple in Jerusalem, Luke's favourite city, in all its splendour. We allow ourselves to become aware of the Trinity into whom we have been baptized. How happily they look upon Jesus as he speaks about God's loving mercy. We may delay as long as we wish in their presence, opening our hearts to admire their wisdom and to drink in their love. How happily they look upon the tax collector. How do they view the 'religious man', the Pharisee? How do they view me as I endeavour to deepen my baptismal relationship with them through my contemplation?

We focus upon Jesus, who recounts this parable under the loving gaze of the Trinity. There are just the two persons and their respective prayers left for us to contemplate. I look at the finely robed Pharisee, and hear the words of his prayer. Surely this is a caricature by Luke. No one could be as stupid as this man in losing touch with God to the degree where he spends his time of prayer in self-congratulation, and in comparisons that denigrate everyone else, especially the other man in the temple, praying with him.

What of the tax collector? His job is one dominated by extortion rackets, and he has reached a time of conversion which brings him to the Temple to pray in humility and simplicity a very brief prayer: 'God, be merciful to me, a sinner.' In the brevity of his prayer he is not alone.

In all of the stories of confession and repentance in the gospels the confessions are always very brief, even non-existent. The longest of them is by the prodigal son: 'Father I have sinned against heaven and before you; I am no longer worthy to be called your son.' Even then he is interrupted by his father who doesn't want to hear speeches but to get on with the celebrations (Luke

God, Be Merciful

15:21). The repentant robber on the cross says, 'We indeed have been condemned justly, for we are getting what we deserved for our deeds' (Luke 23:41). Zacchaeus confesses nothing; he simply talks about making reparation. Peter says, 'Lord, you know that I love you' (John 21:15). The woman caught in adultery speaks only three tiny words, 'No one, sir' (John 8:11). The paralytic let down through the roof in Mark chapter 2 says nothing. And the woman in Luke chapter 7 who wept at the feet of Jesus also says nothing.

What does the tax collector say? 'God, be merciful to me, a sinner.' Forty-two years ago I was giving a retreat to a group of twenty boys in Year 9. They were fourteen-year-olds. We listened together to the parable of the Pharisee and the tax collector. I then asked them, 'What do you think the tax collector did? Did he just say his prayer once, then jump up and walk out of the Temple, or did he say it over and over again? What did he do?' For a while they sat there with furrowed brows, then one lad put up his hand. There's always a wisdom figure in such a group. 'Yes', I said, 'what did he do?' He said, 'I think he went into the Temple, and said it once ... then ... he sort of ... kind of ... you know ...' And I did know.

The boy obviously knew what contemplation was, and that the tax collector was being contemplative in a deep prayer of the heart in God's presence. He simply did not have the concepts or words to express what he knew. And he was right! I think that day a seed was sown that led many years later to the writing of this book.

The tax collector simply acknowledged before God his sinfulness. Acknowledgment is a powerful word. It means taking responsibility *for*. Without trying to excuse myself, to blame someone else, I take ownership of my sin. It is the attitude of David in Psalm 51: 'Against you, you alone, have I sinned, and done what is evil in your sight' (verse 4). In the penitential rite at the Eucharist the priest calls us to acknowledge our sins (*Agnoscamus peccata nostra*). Sadly, it used to be mistranslated into English, 'Let us call to mind our sins.'

The history of the sacrament of penance or reconciliation has been long and extremely varied over the centuries. In the past it has been well taught that there are four essential parts to the sacrament: contrition, confession, absolution and penance.

Of these the first, contrition, is pre-eminent in importance. It seems strange then that the sacrament is most often referred to as 'confession' and priests speak of their role as 'hearing confessions'. This is because psychologically that part of the sacrament looms large and tends to capture the penitent's attention.

Our friend the tax collector was not led astray. He knew that what should win his attention was his relationship with the all-merciful God. This relationship is only accessible through that prayer which we call contemplation. So, when he came to the Temple to pray, he went straight to the heart of the matter and prayed, 'God, be merciful to me a sinner.' The comment of Jesus was that he 'went home justified' rather than the Pharisee.

It is said in jest that many people on hearing this parable often think, 'Thank God I'm not like that Pharisee.' Rather we ought to recognize that there is something of the Pharisee as well as the tax collector in all of us and pray that the Lord moves us more in the direction of the contemplative prayer of the tax collector.

We are the most blessed among all people. As Jesus says in the gospel of John, he has kept no secrets hidden from us. He has revealed everything he has learnt from his Father. The most important thing he has learnt is that God is Love.

Here we are in the presence of the Father, Son and Holy Spirit who look upon each one of us with absolute compassion. All I have to do to know myself to be totally forgiven is to pray the prayer of the tax collector. Can I not do that much? If it is a struggle, Mary and Jesus are here to help me.

— 11 —
Come on Down

Jesus entered Jericho and was passing through it. There was a man there named Zacchaeus; he was a chief tax collector and was very rich. He was trying to see who Jesus was, but on account of the crowd, he could not because he was very short. So he ran ahead and climbed a sycamore tree to see Jesus, because he was going to pass that way. When Jesus came to the place, he looked up and said to him, 'Zacchaeus, hurry and come down; for I must stay at your house today.' So he hurried down and was happy to welcome him.

All who saw it began to grumble and said, 'He has gone to be the guest of one who is a sinner.' Zacchaeus stood there and said to the Lord, 'Look, half of my possessions, Lord, I will give to the poor; and if I have defrauded anyone of anything, I will pay back four times as much.' Then Jesus said to him, 'Today salvation has come to this house, because he too is a son of Abraham. For the Son of Man came to seek out and to save the lost.'

Luke 19:1-10

THIS IS OUR GOSPEL READING for the 31st Sunday of Ordinary Time, Year C, and for the Tuesday of the 33rd week of the year.

As usual, I compose myself for prayer by recalling that I am in the presence of the risen Lord Jesus, who wants to communicate with me through this mystery of his meeting with

Zacchaeus. I am in the company, too, of the Father and the Holy Spirit in whose presence the meeting of Jesus with Zacchaeus is carried out. It can be very helpful to use my imagination to see the road, the crowd, the tree, Jesus and Zacchaeus.

I begin, too, with the ancient prayer of St Richard of Chichester (13th century): 'Thanks be to you, my Lord Jesus Christ, for all the benefits you have given me, for all the pains and insults you have borne for me. Most merciful Redeemer, Friend and Brother, may I know you more clearly, love you more dearly and follow you more nearly.'

I now read through the passage twice, slowly and reflectively, pausing for as long as I wish at anything that strikes me particularly. Some of the following reflections may help.

I may simply rest in the presence of Jesus as he enters the very ancient Jewish walled city of Jericho. I wonder how he is feeling. Is he anticipating any great event that might take place in that city? I ask him.

Zacchaeus appears. I may want to talk to him, to ask him how he is feeling, perhaps to tell him that I too am hoping to have an encounter with Jesus as he did. Hopefully I too experience the same desire as Zacchaeus really to see Jesus. Zacchaeus was rich. I am also rich, maybe not in terms of my bank account, but certainly in the many ways that God is blessing me in my life.

Now we have the dramatic event of Zacchaeus running ahead and climbing a tree; he really wants to see Jesus. Do I? Hopefully I find myself up a tree as Jesus comes to the spot and stops. Then comes the key to the whole of this contemplation: Jesus calls me by name, as he did Zacchaeus, and says to me, 'Hurry and come down.' Do not be surprised if you find it very difficult to carry out this instruction. Coming down means leaving the comfort zone of my tree; it means being exposed to the stares of the crowd. It means a face to face encounter with Jesus, looking into his eyes and he into mine. It may well take me a long time to leave my tree and enter into this meeting with Jesus.

But when I do come down; what do I experience? Love, compassion and mercy. The taunt of the crowd – 'He has gone to be the guest of one who is a sinner' – not only does not hurt me, but is really a compliment to me. My sin is totally forgiven and forgotten. I hear the words of Jesus, 'I must stay at your house today.' I am reminded of his words in John's gospel, 'Those who love me will keep my word, and my Father will love them, and we will come to them and make our home with them' (John 14:23).

Having experienced the Lord's overwhelming mercy and love, I am invited, like Zacchaeus, to make my response. Zacchaeus gives us a very good, twofold example: first, of practical charity to those in need, and, second, of making practical reparation to those we have hurt. It could be wonderful to take time out to perhaps make a list of people whom we have hurt or offended, and then to be on the lookout for opportunities to do them some special kindness, hopefully practical, but at least in word, or in prayer, on their behalf.

The final outcome of this mystery and of our prayer is that the Lord has indeed sought out and saved someone who, without his intervention, was lost. So, hopefully, filled with gratitude, I spend some time in thanking Jesus, as well as the Father, Son and Holy Spirit.

— 12 —
Do Not Sin Again

Early in the morning Jesus came again to the Temple. All the people came to him, and he sat down and began to teach them. The scribes and the Pharisees brought a woman who been caught in adultery; and, making her stand there before all of them, they said to him, 'Teacher, this woman was caught in the very act of committing adultery. Now, in the law Moses commanded us to stone such women. What do you say?' They said this to test him, so that they might have some charge to bring against him.

Jesus bent down and wrote with his finger on the ground. When they kept on questioning him, he straightened and said to them, 'Let anyone among you who is without sin be the first to throw a stone at her.' And once again he bent down and wrote on the ground.

When they heard it they went away, one by one, beginning with the elders; and Jesus was left alone with the woman standing before him. Jesus looked up and said to her, 'Woman, where are they? Has no one condemned you?' She said, 'No one, sir.' And Jesus said, 'Neither do I condemn you. Go your way, and from now on do not sin again.'

John 8:2-11

THIS IS THE GOSPEL READING for the 5th Sunday of Lent, Year C, a year in which the regular Lenten gospels are taken from the gospel of Luke. Perhaps the liturgists have bowed to the opinion of some scripture scholars that this is part of Luke's gospel which has somehow become displaced into the text of John's gospel. Whatever about that, we receive it as a powerful statement of the compassion of Jesus and his forgiving love of which we all stand in need.

The first two verses provide us with a very fitting *mise-en-scène* for our contemplation. Their simplicity conveys a sense of peace and calm as we observe Jesus seated among the people in his teaching role. We may like to stay and gaze at him in contemplation. It will be soon enough for the tumult that is about to break out.

All of sudden the peace is shattered by the arrival of the 'gang' of scribes and Pharisees, dragging along the poor unfortunate woman, and forcing her to stand in her humiliation 'in full view of everybody'. Already our author has communicated a striking picture of the woman being totally outnumbered and hounded by this gang of bigger, older, physically stronger, authoritarian men.

Now the gang turns its attention to Jesus, with one of their typical, often repeated entrapment challenges based on the Mosaic law. In their pathetic two-sentence address they really give themselves away, 'Master, this woman was caught in the very act of committing adultery.' Who staked out her house? Peered through the window?

How does Jesus respond? In silence he bends down to write on the ground. His posture is not far removed from his original posture of being seated, gently instructing the people. He ignores the direct challenge and the question of the scribes and Pharisees. Like many a politician he refuses to be trapped by their aggressive demands.

Perhaps unconsciously they have set up a dilemma the resolution of which is to be found only in their own humanness with its God-given compassion and mercy. It is as if Jesus is allowing them time to get in touch with this, if it has not been irrevocably lost.

What of the woman? Surely the quiet gentle peace emanating from Jesus is not lost on her. What a contrast with her earlier feeling of being overwhelmed and hounded by the bullying mob.

In their curiosity, scripture scholars over the centuries have loved to speculate on what it was Jesus may have written on the ground! Probably the best answer is – 'nothing in particular; he simply doodled.' The whole point is about his posture; he is now lower, nearer to the earth, than the woman – the only one who puts himself in this position! His bending down and the delaying tactics of the doodling allow time to begin to take some of the heat out of the situation. That heat is then totally blown away by his famous words, 'If there is one of you who has not sinned, let him be the first to throw a stone at her.' Slowly the message sinks in; one by one they walk away.

Now the scene is ready for the essence of our contemplation: Jesus alone with the woman, she standing and he in the lower position, still bent over his doodling. The creation of this scene was the whole reason why he bent down in the first place. He looks up to her! Now Jesus speaks to the woman, ever so briefly. 'Has no one condemned you?' There is no question of enquiring if this has happened before, or of asking what other sins she has committed.

What of the woman's 'confession'? In the whole drama she speaks only three words: surely the shortest confession of all time, 'No one, sir.' 'Neither do I condemn you.' Jesus replies. He never does. I may like to stay in his presence in gratitude for the total forgiveness of all my sins that comes to me again as I contemplate this Lenten gospel.

Jesus concludes this wonderfully wrought story with the words, 'Do not sin again.' How sad if anyone were to hear these words as an imposition, another injunction. In effect Jesus is saying to me, as to the woman, 'Remember the love of this encounter, and you won't sin again.' We can rest assured she went on her way with a heart filled with peace and joy. May we also.

For the woman, the joy and the peace she now feels come from her experience of being totally forgiven through the total acceptance of the one who never condemns but loves without reservation. May we too come to that same peace and joy through this contemplation. I may like to conclude my time of prayer by entering into conversation with Mary, with Jesus and with the woman.

— 13 —

Be Forgiving as Your Heavenly Father Is Forgiving

Then Peter came and said to Jesus, 'Lord, if my brother sins against me, how often should I forgive? As many as seven times?' Jesus said to him, 'Not seven times, I tell you, but seventy-seven times.

'For this reason the kingdom of heaven may be compared to a king who wished to settle accounts with his slaves. When he began the reckoning, one who owed him ten thousand talents was brought to him; and, as he could not pay, his lord ordered him to be sold, together with his wife and children and all his possessions, and payment to be made. So the slave fell on his knees before him, saying, "Have patience with me, and I will pay you everything." And out of pity for him, the lord of that slave released him and forgave him the debt. But the same slave, as he went out, came upon one of his fellow slaves who owed him a hundred denarii; and seizing him by the throat, he said, "Pay me what you owe me." Then his fellow slave fell down and pleaded with him, "Have patience and I will pay you." But he refused; then he went and threw him into prison until he would pay the debt.

'When his fellow slaves saw what had happened, they were greatly distressed, and they went and reported to their lord all that had taken place. Then his lord summoned him and said to him, "You wicked slave! I forgave you all that debt because you pleaded with me. Should you not have had

Be Forgiving as Your Heavenly Father Is Forgiving

mercy upon your fellow slave, as I had mercy on you?" And in anger his lord handed him over to be tortured until he would pay his entire debt. So my heavenly Father will do to every one of you, if you do not forgive your brother or sister from your heart.'

Matthew 18:21-35

THIS IS THE GOSPEL for the 24th Sunday of Ordinary Time (Year A) and Tuesday of the 3rd week of Lent. The text provides a most important and fruitful subject for our contemplation.

As we enter upon our prayer, it is not difficult to fix the eyes of our imagination upon Jesus and upon Peter, who in his typical extrovert style detaches himself from the other disciples because he has something to get off his chest. We can well imagine that Peter's question about the number of times he should forgive is not a theoretical one, but one concerned with some real personal relationship of his.

Moreover, Peter surely imagines that he would be very generous in offering to forgive as many as seven times. But Jesus replies by raising the argument to a totally new level. He points to God's forgiving love which knows no limits whatever. Matthew's 'seventy-seven times' implies this total lack of limitation. In some texts it reads seventy times seven times, and in Luke (the great gospel of compassion and forgiveness) 'seven times a day'! In other words, for Jesus our forgiveness must be modelled on God's forgiveness, which knows no limits.

Faced with the impossibility of being like God in the extent of our forgiving, we must turn to prayer for God's grace, which can do for us what is humanly impossible. The reception of this grace then becomes for Jesus the point of the parable which follows. Jesus stresses the point of the infinity of God's forgiveness by naming the amount the master forgives the wicked servant as approximately $20 million! The amount the wicked servant subsequently fails to forgive his fellow servant is then a paltry $25! Though the figures mentioned seem to us fantastic, they are surpassed by the realities of God's forgiveness and our refusal to forgive. God forgives us not just seven times a day, but always, even at the cost of sending God's only Son to live and die on our behalf.

Far beyond any question of our drawing a moral from the parable, or our making a resolution to be more forgiving is what happens in the authentic reception of God's grace. When, through contemplation, we know in our heart the gift of God's totally forgiving love, we receive the grace to be totally forgiving of everyone else. We find that the spirit of resentment and criticism of the behaviour of others has disappeared from our heart.

What an extraordinary change such a conversion works in people. They can, to the surprise of others who may have had them pigeon-holed, grow out of lifelong habits of always blaming someone else for any of their perceived faults. They can be healed from deep-seated attitudes of always being 'agin the government', or their parents, spouse, children, neighbours. They are truly set free. Could this happen to me in so far as I am in need of it? Yes, it can.

St Paul had this experience, and summed it up in Galatians 2:20: 'It is no longer I who live, but it is Christ who lives in me. And the life I now live in the flesh I live by faith in the Son of God, who loved me and gave himself for me.' Like Paul, knowing myself as a forgiven sinner, I will find it impossible not to forgive any perceived hurts or faults that come from anyone else.

The Gospel teaching of God's infinite forgiveness and of the call to every Christian to live out that same profound attitude of forgiveness is absolutely central to Christianity. Luke concludes his great teaching about love of enemies (Luke 6:27-36) with the words, 'Be compassionate as your heavenly Father is compassionate.' Not only do Luke and Matthew include our prayer for a forgiving heart in the Lord's Prayer, but Matthew goes as far as to instruct us to leave our gift at the altar, go and be reconciled with anyone who has something against us, and then return to offer our gift. (Matthew 5:24).

The role of forgiveness in our lives is essential in all human relationships. Perhaps this is why it is so important for married people, as they fulfil their vocation to mutual love, continually to practise the call to mutual admission of fault and mutual forgiveness.

Our human forgiveness is truly a God-like quality, and is clearly an example of grace directly at work in us. We can only forgive one another if we know the power and mercy of the forgiveness we have received from God. The acceptance of God's total forgiveness is the central, pivotal grace of Christian spirituality. All our life of virtue and service of one another is only possible if we are able to draw on the profound spiritual strength of the knowledge of God's personal love for me.

We see, then, how Jesus turns Peter's question about his own responsibility and moral behaviour into a contemplation of the infinite forgiving love of the Father. To the question about 'seven times' the real answer is always.

God never condemns. God always forgives – totally. To experience this, all I need to do is to take on board through contemplation the repeated saying of the first letter of John: 'God is love' (1 John 4:8; 4:16). Matthew's great parable is a powerful illustration of what Isaiah wrote, 'Though your sins are as scarlet, they shall be as white as snow; though they are as red as crimson, they shall be like wool' (Isaiah 1:18). To know this as a heart experience I have to rely solely on divine grace and mercy.

Hence the supreme importance in a contemplation of this kind of entering into earnest conversation with my intercessors, Mary and Jesus and my other friends, and with the Holy Spirit, the Son and the Father, as I pray for the grace to know myself as a totally loved and forgiven sinner.

— 14 —
An Advent Contemplation

In those days, John the Baptist appeared in the wilderness of Judea, proclaiming, 'Repent, for the kingdom of heaven has come near.' This is the one of whom the prophet spoke when he said, 'The voice of one crying in the wilderness, "Prepare the way of the Lord, make his paths straight."'

Now John wore clothing of camel's hair with a leather belt round his waist, and his food was locusts and wild honey. Then the people of Jerusalem and all Judea were going out to him, and all the region along the Jordan, and they were baptized by him in the river Jordan, confessing their sins.

But when he saw many Pharisees and Sadducees coming for baptism, he said to them, 'You brood of vipers! Who warned you to flee from the wrath to come? Bring forth fruit worthy of repentance. Do not presume to say to yourselves, "We have Abraham as our ancestor"; for God is able from these stones to raise up children to Abraham. Even now the axe is lying at the root of the trees; every tree therefore that does not bear good fruit is cut down and thrown into the fire. I baptize you with water for repentance, but the one who is more powerful than I is coming after me; I am not worthy to carry his sandals. He will baptize you with the Holy Spirit and fire. His winnowing fork is in his hand, and he will clear his threshing floor and will gather his wheat into the granary; but the chaff he will burn with unquenchable fire.'

Matthew 3:1-12

THIS IS OUR GOSPEL READING for the 2nd Sunday of Advent, Year A.

After the 'link Sunday' of the first of Advent, repeating the eschatological themes of the end of the year readings, this second Sunday introduces the two great Advent heroes, Isaiah and John the Baptist. The first reading, from Isaiah, promises the glorious future to be brought about for Israel by a descendant of Jesse. When the gospel focuses our attention on John, once again it is Isaiah who is quoted as revealing to us who John is, 'a voice crying in the wilderness: Prepare a way for the Lord, make his paths straight.'

As we begin our prayer, in the presence of the Trinity – and a careful reflective making of the Sign of the Cross is an excellent way of providing this setting – we are invited to focus on the person of John. We already know him from the infancy gospels as the cousin of Jesus. Now we see him as the grown man, strong, ascetic and fearlessly prophetic. Our text gives a clear picture to fill our imagination: 'living rough' in both clothing and diet.

John very probably belonged to the contemporary Essene community east of Jordan, but is now presented on an individual mission of preaching and baptising. His person captures the imagination of 'the people of Jerusalem and all Judaea and the whole Jordan district'.

Perhaps I, too, can allow myself to be drawn by the attraction of this truly authentic ascetic. People find a powerful appeal in a radical and simple lifestyle as a sign of total commitment to spiritual reality and truth. There is nothing of the false philosophy of the Greek Stoics in John, but rather a freedom based on a deep relationship with God, not just the God of the Old Testament, but with 'the one who is to come, whose sandal I am not fit to carry, who will baptize you with Holy Spirit and with fire.' This kind of freedom can provide me with a welcome release from the cloying clutter of our modern living.

As always, when we contemplate, presence to a person – in this case John the Baptist – can so capture our attention that we can simply stay via our imagination with that person for the whole of our prayer time, gazing, admiring, perhaps entering into conversation. If we desire to move on, we listen to the words of that person.

What wonderful words we have here: 'Repent, for the kingdom of heaven is close at hand.' The whole of creation, the whole of human history has been preparing, through the infinite patience of our loving God, for this moment in time, for the coming of Christ. When Jesus does come, his message is identical: 'Repent, for the kingdom of God is close at hand' (Mark 1:15). Here we have the twofold theme of Advent: the coming of our God amongst us – 'They will call him Emmanuel, a name which means God-is-with-us' – and repentance.

Every Advent we celebrate three comings of God:

- the obvious coming of God in Jesus at Christmas;
- the promised 'second coming' of Christ as saviour and judge at the end of time;
- the coming of the Lord into our lives today, right here and now.

So all of time, past, present and future, is consecrated by God. Human history, the present moment and the future can all be experienced under the aspect of eternity.

The second great theme of Advent is that of repentance. While this theme is somewhat tempered in Advent by the theme of the Lord's coming, Advent has traditionally ranked with Lent as the two great seasons for turning back to God more deeply, and so preparing for the great celebrations of Christmas and Easter.

Though Lent is more prolonged and more focused in this regard, John's message to the Pharisees and Sadducees, and via them to us, is certainly one of urgency and importance. Inspired by the towering figure of John the Baptist, may we find that this Advent leads us into deeper union with the Lord, our saviour.

Let us ask Mary to obtain for us from her Son the ongoing grace of deep repentance for our sin, as well as a heightened awareness of the Lord's coming. Let us ask Jesus for that same grace, and come again before the Persons of the Trinity, begging each one for this twofold grace.

— 15 —
Go to Joseph

Here we have two readings about the role of Joseph in the lives of Jesus and Mary. The first is the gospel for the solemnity of St Joseph (19 March) and for the 4th Sunday of Advent (Year A), also for 18 December and for Christmas Eve. The second reading is from the Midnight Mass of Christmas.

> Now the birth of Jesus the Messiah took place in this way. When his mother Mary had been engaged to Joseph, but before they lived together, she was found to be with child from the Holy Spirit. Her husband Joseph, being a just man, and unwilling to expose her to public disgrace, planned to dismiss her quietly.
>
> But just when he had resolved to do this, an angel of the Lord appeared to him in a dream and said, 'Joseph, son of David, do not be afraid to take Mary as your wife, for the child conceived in her is from the Holy Spirit. She will bear a son, and you are to name him Jesus, for he will save his people from their sins.' All this took place to fulfil what had been spoken by the Lord through the prophet – 'Look, the virgin shall conceive and bear a son, and they shall call him Emmanuel', which means, 'God is with us.'
>
> When Joseph awoke from sleep, he did as the angel of the Lord commanded him; he took her as his wife, but had no marital relations with her until she had borne a son; and he named him Jesus.
>
> Matthew 1:18-23

In those days a decree went out from Emperor Augustus that all the world should be registered. This was the first registration and was taken while Quirinius was governor of Syria. All went to their own towns to be registered. Joseph also went from the town of Nazareth in Galilee to Judea, to the city of David called Bethlehem, because he was descended from the house and family of David. He went to be registered with Mary, to whom he was engaged and who was expecting a child.

While they were there, the time came for her to deliver her child. And she gave birth to her firstborn son, and wrapped him in bands of cloth, and laid him in a manger, because there was no place for them in the inn.

Luke 2:1-7

IT IS EXTREMELY WORTHWHILE to devote one of our times of contemplation to Joseph, patron of the universal church. St Ignatius of Loyola was very devoted to the saints in general and to many of them personally. See the excerpts from his *Spiritual Journal* below.

'Patron of the universal church' does not, of course, mean that Joseph keeps an eye on a vast crowd of people, but that he is personally and intimately in relationship with each one of us. Joseph has always been seen as the New Testament parallel of Joseph, son of Jacob, whose story is told in the concluding chapters of the book of Genesis. Not only did the Pharaoh make Joseph his deputy as lord of all Egypt, but, when the people approached him with their problems, he would say, 'Go to Joseph', because Joseph had a wonderful personal touch.

That phrase of Pharaoh has repeatedly been invoked by the church as an exhortation to the modern People of God about relating to Joseph. All development in personal relationships takes place in contemplation. May we be helped through our contemplation to come to a deeper and more abiding relationship with this great man.

Apart from the two gospel readings above, along with the readings surrounding the flight into Egypt, there are only a few passing gospel references to Joseph. We learn that Joseph, like Jesus, was a carpenter. We know that he is never quoted, but he is a living example that actions speak louder than words. At the presentation in the Temple, 'the father and mother of Jesus marvelled at what was being said about him [by Simeon]' (Luke 2:33).

We could well delay here with Joseph, the man of contemplation. How constantly he must have marvelled as, hour by hour, day by day, year by year, he lived in the presence of his son. Of course, as in all family life, it was not all sweetness and light. Mary is quoted as saying (Luke 2:48): 'Look, your father and I have been searching for you in great anxiety.'

The first of our readings is the Annunciation of the birth of Jesus. In popular imagination, the term 'annunciation' is used only of the annunciation to Mary in Luke's gospel, the gospel most focused on women. Matthew is writing for a Jewish audience, so he follows the tradition of the Jews that the role of the father is paramount. It is Joseph who names the child Jesus (verse 25). Mary and Joseph were betrothed (verse 18). This is a much stronger than our engagement. They were virtually married, but not yet living together.

What does Joseph make of her pregnancy? Ask him. He is a just man. This is the only comment directly made about a virtue of Joseph in Scripture, though we will see other sterling qualities in his actions. Joseph's justice means much more than law-abiding. He is a truly compassionate man. He loves Mary deeply, so will not shame her. It is at this point that we have the first divine intervention for Joseph in the form of a dream.

There will be two more, surrounding the flight into Egypt. Joseph is fulfilling in his own life the outstanding quality of the Joseph of the book of Genesis, the dreamer and interpreter of dreams.

It is fruitless to spend time speculating about what might have or could have happened historically, but it is legitimate to extrapolate a little. We may well wonder what Joseph the dreamer of dreams may have dreamt of as a future for his small family in the tiny town of Nazareth. Like any father, he had his waking dreams, but whatever they were the cruel hand of circumstances overtook them.

According to Luke, a census suddenly demanded a long and arduous journey to Bethlehem. All the careful preparations for the birth must be abandoned. Joseph was an obedient man and a man of action. After the annunciation, as soon as he woke from sleep, 'he did as the angel of the Lord commanded him' (Matthew 1:24). The same will be true after each of the two angelic dreams before fleeing to Egypt and before returning (Matthew 2:13, 19).

At Bethlehem Mary gave birth to a son and placed him in a feeding trough for animals, because there was no room in the inn. There is no hint of rejection or of harsh treatment. It is simply a fact that the inn is full. Joseph is not mentioned. He is a truly humble man. We can enter in imagination into seeing the silent figure in the background, into conversing with him, asking about his feelings, contemplating this contemplative, compassionate, loving, silent, humble, dreaming man. What a model for fathers he is!

— 16 —

The Annunciation to Mary

In the sixth month, the angel Gabriel was sent by God to a town in Galilee called Nazareth to a virgin engaged to a man whose name was Joseph, of the house of David. The virgin's name was Mary. He came to her and said, 'Greetings, favoured one! The Lord is with you.'

But she was much perplexed by his words and pondered what sort of greeting this might be. The angel said to her, 'Do not be afraid, Mary, for you have found favour with God. And, now, you will conceive in your womb, and bear a son, and you will name him Jesus. He will be great, and will be called the Son of the Most High, and the Lord God will give to him the throne of his ancestor David. He will reign over the house of Jacob forever, and of his kingdom there will be no end.'

Mary said to the angel, 'How can this be, since I am a virgin?' The angel said to her, 'The Holy Spirit will come upon you, and the power of the Most High will overshadow you; therefore the child to be born will be holy; he will be called Son of God. And, now, your relative Elizabeth in her old age has also conceived a son; and this is the sixth month for her who was said to be barren. For nothing will be impossible with God.'

And Mary said, 'Here I am, the handmaid of the Lord; let it be with me according to your word.' Then the angel departed from her.

Luke 1:26-38

COME, LORD JESUS

HERE WE HAVE for our contemplation what is clearly one of the most beautiful stories of Luke the great story teller. We are led to contemplate the intimate process of Mary's 'yes' to God, as well as the moment in our history when in the Incarnation the Word was made flesh. This gospel is read on the solemnities of the Annunciation and the Immaculate Conception, as well as on the 4th Sunday of Advent, Year B, and 20 December.

Luke begins his story very simply, almost laconically, as he situates his story in the context of the annunciation to Zechariah of the birth of John the Baptist and Elizabeth's subsequent pregnancy. It all happens in the sixth month. Luke goes on to give us the geographical context, 'to a town in Galilee called Nazareth'. Only then are we introduced to Joseph, to king David, and finally to Mary. God's message to Mary, via the angelic visitor, is a most positive one: 'Greetings, favoured one!'

Perhaps for us Mary's response is surprising. Obviously, in her humility she had never regarded herself as highly favoured. Here she is, a frail, teenage girl, in a 'nothing' village in the remote province of Galilee. So she is 'much perplexed' at the greeting, and in her puzzlement tries to find in her own mind what it might mean.

Already Mary is presented to us as a reflective, contemplative kind of person. We could be excused in thinking Gabriel had been swotting up on the prophet Isaiah before making this visit: 'Do not be afraid; I am with you; I call you by your name; you are mine' (Isaiah 43:1). Then, in the felicitous translation of the Jerusalem Bible, comes the often repeated exhortation of Isaiah – 'Listen!' – followed by the annunciation of Mary's coming pregnancy and the birth of one who is to be called Jesus ('the Lord is saviour').

This child is to have four marks of greatness:

The Annunciation to Mary

- He will be called Son of the Most High.
- The Lord God will give him the throne of his father, David.
- He will reign over the house of Jacob forever.
- Of his kingdom there will be no end.

Is this enough to convince Mary?

Once again, the reflectivity and contemplation of Mary emerges. Great statements do not sway her. She rightly objects that she is not yet formally married and living with her husband. Clearly from the whole drift of the interview so far the pregnancy is being proposed as imminent. In answer to Mary's question – 'How can this be, since I have no husband?' – Gabriel's language and manner change to the profoundly spiritual: 'The Holy Spirit will come upon you, and the power of the Most High will overshadow you; therefore the child to be born will be called holy, the Son of God.'

This statement, of course, cannot be construed to mean that the Holy Spirit is the father of the child. Just in case this is not enough to convince Mary and win her 'yes', Gabriel has a final trump up his sleeve. After giving the news of Elizabeth's unexpected pregnancy, he produces the trump card: 'Nothing will be impossible with God.'

Mary said: 'Here I am, the handmaid of the Lord; let it be with me according to your word.' Here we have the perfect model of response. Not only have all the preliminaries in the interview revealed in Mary a person of profound discernment, but the whole tone of her response reveals she recognizes that all power and initiative must come from the Lord. Her perfect human response is primarily passive – 'Let it be with me.' At the same time it calls upon all of Mary's human potential and commitment for it to happen.

It is most appropriate at this moment, as we contemplate

Mary, that we should stay with her and ask her to help us join in this whole-hearted response to God in our lives. This response of ours is not only a general accepting of God's will, but there may also be some particular aspect of our lives in which we experience the here and now need to say 'yes' to God.

It is so clear from this wonderful narrative, worthy of repeated contemplation, that true cooperation with God comes from a gift of the Holy Spirit deep within us, engaging all the characteristics and potential of each individual person.

At that moment, the Word was made Flesh. Luke then summarily writes, 'the angel departed from her.' Immediately after that Mary began the long journey to Judea to assist Elizabeth in her pregnancy. The Mary we met in our contemplation of the Annunciation remains essentially practical and down to earth. Even in our most contemplative moments life must go on.

17

Our Life of Hope

When the time came for their purification, Joseph and Mary brought Jesus up to Jerusalem to present him to the Lord, and offer a sacrifice according to what is stated in the law of the Lord, 'a pair of turtledoves or two young pigeons'.

Now there was a man in Jerusalem whose name was Simeon; this man was righteous and devout, looking forward to the consolation of Israel, and the Holy Spirit rested on him. It had been revealed to him by the Holy Spirit that he would not see death before he had seen the Lord's Messiah. Guided by the Spirit, Simeon came into the Temple; and when the parents brought in the child Jesus, to do for him what was customary under the law, Simeon took him in his arms and praised God, saying, 'Master, now you are dismissing your servant in peace, according to your word; for my eyes have seen your salvation, which you have prepared in the presence of all peoples, a light for revelation to the Gentiles and for glory to your people Israel.'

And the child's father and mother were amazed at what was being said about him. Then Simeon blessed them and said to his mother Mary, 'This child is destined for the falling and the rising of many in Israel, and to be a sign that will be opposed so that the inner thoughts of many will be revealed – and a sword will pierce your own soul too.'

There was also a prophet, Anna, the daughter of Phanuel, of the tribe of Asher. She was of a great age, having lived with her husband seven years after her marriage, then as a widow to the age of eighty-four. She never left the Temple but worshipped there with fasting and prayer night and day. At that moment she came, and began to praise God and to speak about the child to all who were looking for the redemption of Jerusalem.

Luke 2:22-38

IN OUR LITURGY, this gospel, besides being read on the feasts of the Presentation of the Lord (2 February) and of the Holy Family (Year 2), appears also on 29-30 December.

Perhaps no other part of the New Testament better captures the spirit of Advent than the story of the presentation of the baby Jesus in the Temple. As we take it up for a time of contemplation, it should not be difficult to focus our attention. Our imagination is immediately captured by the magnificence of the white marble Temple, as well as by the persons in the story – Jesus himself who does only what babies do, Joseph, Mary, Simeon, Anna, and the many other worshippers and bystanders.

As I focus on them, I may be struck by their joy at this ceremony, by their simplicity and poverty (perhaps in contrast to the rich, making more magnificent offerings), their spirit of gratitude, and maybe above all the overriding atmosphere of hope that comes with a new human life, and the expectation of a glorious future.

The two persons Luke gives close attention to in this story are Simeon and Anna. They are both old (though only Anna's age is specifically mentioned), with all the feebleness and dependence of the elderly. They represent the *Anawim*, who are so dear to Luke. 'Happy are you who are poor, for yours is the kingdom of heaven' (Luke 6:20). They have nothing to look forward to except the liberation of Israel that the longed-for Messiah is to bring.

Their presence in the Temple (constant in Anna's case) is the sign of this longing. The poverty they experience opens them up to that other presence so dear to Luke, that of the Holy Spirit. This presence leads to a profound acceptance of the gift of Wisdom, so characteristic of the elderly. Simeon is enabled to bestow blessings, and Anna to be prophetic.

We are eternally grateful to Simeon for his famous canticle the *Nunc dimittis*: 'Now, Lord, you dismiss your servant in peace ...' It shows us a profound contemplative acceptance of the mystery of life and death, a true wisdom of the elderly.

These qualities of Simeon and Anna are, of course, to be found at a more eminent level in Luke's other two great characters, Mary and Joseph. They do not speak, except through their silence, but they are the ones whose whole lives are focused on the presence of the baby in their arms who is the living sign of hope for salvation, not only for the people of Israel, and for the 'nations' of Simeon's great hymn, but for the whole world, and indeed for the whole of creation.

Mary's unique response to the Father's love – 'Let it happen to me according to your word' (Luke 1:38) – makes her the living sign of hope in her Son for all who will come after her. Their attitude comes from a profound sense of what Paul will later express: 'However many promises God made, the Yes to them all is in him [the Lord Jesus]' (2 Corinthians 1:20). Or, as the letter to the Colossians puts it, 'the mystery is Christ among you, your hope of glory' (Colossians 1:27).

Over the five centuries since the return of Israel from exile in Babylon there had been a constant succession of Simeons and Annas, God's poor and holy ones, whose whole life was lived in prayer and worship and expectation of the coming of the

Messiah. What of these nameless ones and their seemingly unfulfilled hopes? The fulfilment of hope comes not only in a sudden one-off revelation as it did for Simeon and Anna, but in the waiting itself, in the commitment and patience of those others.

In the long hours of contemplation God's promise is fulfilled, not in an external event, but in a profound attitude of heart in the Lord's hidden presence. We could fulfil our own desires to capture the hope that this Advent brings by contemplating the persons of Mary, Joseph, Simeon and Anna, and entering into conversation with each of them.

— 18 —
Jesus Is Baptized

In those days, Jesus came from Nazareth of Galilee and was baptized by John in the Jordan. And just as he was coming up out of the water, he saw the heavens torn apart and the Spirit descending like a dove upon him. And a voice came from heaven, 'You are my Son, the beloved; with you I am well pleased.'

Mark 1:7-11

THIS GOSPEL IS READ on the Feast of the Baptism of the Lord, Year B, and on the weekday of 6 January.

Our contemplation of the Lord's Baptism takes us to the heart of one of the greatest mysteries of the life of Jesus. While the Incarnation and every mystery following it up to this point have each their own unique importance, now the time has come for Jesus to enter formally, explicitly and publicly on the great mission the Father has planned for the salvation of our race. It is important, then, for each of us to enter solemnly into this saving mission, using the introductory steps outlined in Appendix A (see pp. 192-198).

It can be very helpful to take time to reflect on the departure of Jesus from his home in Nazareth of Galilee. This is probably the only time Jesus has left home in his thirty-six years apart from his trip to Jerusalem at the age of twelve. I can stay with the parting, so moving because there is a strong sense that he will never return. I watch him hug Mary his mother, and Joseph his father, if I choose to believe Joseph is still alive, and his close relatives. Then he is gone. I may want to stay for some time with Mary and Joseph, in prayer with them.

Now I am alone with Jesus as he walks deliberately on his long journey to the place on the Jordan where John is baptizing. As he walks Jesus is alone, but far from alone. Father, eternal Son and Holy Spirit are with him every step of the way, as they will be with him in every one of the gospel mysteries that we contemplate. He lives always under their loving gaze.

When Jesus approaches John for baptism, which was a sign of repentance, in union with the sinful people, John protests, but Jesus, in his identification with his sinful brothers and sisters, prevails.

What happens next takes us right into the heart of this mystery. There is a revelation of the Father and of the Holy Spirit present with Jesus. The Spirit appears in the form of a dove, that very gentle bird which is a traditional symbol of peace. Though the public life of Jesus will be exteriorly anything but peaceful, his heart is here truly at profound peace because of his union with the Trinity. Through my baptism I share that same union, and am called to the same profound peace of heart.

The principal element of this mystery of the Lord's baptism is the voice of the Father which proclaims to Jesus, 'You are my Son, the beloved; with you I am well pleased.' Here Mark uses the first line of Isaiah 42:1, the first of the four poems of the Suffering Servant of the Lord, which go right through to our Good Friday reading of chapters 52-53. Notice that Mark deliberately changes the saying from the third person – 'This is my Son' – to the second person – 'You are my Son' – and in this is followed by Luke. Matthew, in his Jewish faithfulness to the original of Isaiah, retains the third person. Jesus is clearly marked as beginning his public mission as one of suffering in the service of the Father.

Jesus Is Baptized

We should be very grateful to Mark that for him the Father's affirmation of love is directed personally to Jesus. He is strengthened and energized for carrying out his suffering mission by hearing at depth the Father's loving words addressed to him to send him forth on that mission. Later, in Acts 10:38, in his address in the house of Cornelius, Peter gives a wonderful commentary on this: '... how God anointed Jesus of Nazareth with the Holy Spirit and with power; how he went about doing good and healing all who were oppressed by the devil, for God was with him.'

As I contemplate the Father's empowering word to Jesus, I too am invited to hear the Father say to me right here and now, 'You are my beloved son/daughter; with you I am well pleased.' I can stay for a long time basking in this affirmation of the Father's personal love for me.

My contemplation of this mystery of Jesus takes me right into the heart of the basic mystery of Salvation History. I am not taking an imaginary journey 2000 years back in time. I am relating to the saving mystery of the risen Lord inviting me to join him on his here and now mission to bring salvation to people desperately in need of it. I am relating to the saving action of the Trinity in my world today. As this happens, I may be moved to speak to any of the persons I have met in this contemplation: to Mary, to Joseph, Jesus, John the Baptist, the Father, the Son, the Spirit.

In doing this, I fulfil St Teresa's definition of contemplation as 'a close sharing between friends'.

— 19 —

Jesus Is Tempted

Jesus, full of the Holy Spirit, returned from the Jordan and was led by the Spirit in the wilderness, where for forty days he was tempted by the devil. He ate nothing at all during those days, and when they were over he was famished. The devil said to him, 'If you are the Son of God, command this stone to become a loaf of bread.' Jesus answered him, 'It is written, "One does not live by bread alone."'

Then the devil led him up and showed him in an instant all the kingdoms of the world. And the devil said to him, 'To you I will give their glory and all this authority; for it has been given over to me, and I give it to anyone I please. If you, then, will worship me, it will all be yours.' Jesus answered him, 'It is written, "Worship the Lord your God, and serve only him."'

Then the devil took him to Jerusalem, and placed him on the pinnacle of the Temple, saying to him, 'If you are the Son of God, throw yourself down, for it is written, "He will command his angels concerning you, to protect you", and "On their hands they will bear you up so that you will not dash your foot against a stone."' Jesus answered him, 'It is said, "Do not put the Lord your God to the test."'

When the devil finished every test, he departed from him until an opportune time.

Luke 4:1-13

Jesus Is Tempted

Each year our gospel reading for the first Sunday of Lent focuses on the temptations of Jesus in the desert. For Year C the reading is from Luke's gospel.

I may find it helpful to compose myself for prayer by taking a posture that is both alert and relaxed; it may also help to take a few deep breaths and to become very aware of my breathing; it will certainly help to remember that the Jesus whom I wish to contemplate is living within me by faith and through my baptism. I may wish to begin to speak with him and to ask for what I desire during this time of prayer.

As I begin to reflect on the temptation story as told by Mark, Matthew and Luke, I remind myself of the great text of the letter to the Hebrews 4:15, 'Jesus was tempted in every respect as we are, but without sin.' The story of his temptations is the story of the basic temptations of our humanness by which the spirit of evil tries to lead us astray.

First, there is the temptation to satisfy immediate needs, to misuse God's creation, by turning stones into bread. Jesus could not only alleviate his own extreme hunger, but also feed all the poor by turning huge rocks into bread! The temptations are each concerned with false ways of attempting to bring about the coming of God's Kingdom.

Second, there is the big lie; surely Jesus could not possibly fall for the devil's ploy of worshipping him and so winning all the kingdoms of the world! Yet human history is riddled with cases of people making 'a deal with the devil'.

Third, 'Jump from the top of the Temple.' Here is a clever, quick and easy way of capturing attention – with a view to the good purpose of making the kingdom come, perhaps a way that would appeal to many a modern advertiser!

The gospel of Matthew follows the logical order of the three temptations, moving through the three levels of depth – from satisfying hunger, to winning popular acclaim, to making the pact with the devil. Luke reverses the order of the second and third, to focus the reader's attention on Jerusalem as the climax of the whole story, Jerusalem being of supreme importance in the whole structure of Luke's gospel.

We are called to awareness, to recognize the fundamental downward spiral on which evil tries to lead us: from wanting to possess material things in a way that does not respect them but uses them to feed our ego, to wanting other people's attention in a way that feeds that same ego, to wanting power to control all of reality and to control other persons.

The radical nature of the story of the three temptations of Jesus is brought out in the consideration that it is the story of the reversal of the sin of Adam and Eve. The devil tempted them to abdicate their humanness by wanting to be 'like gods'. Jesus who is God refuses to act as God because he totally embraces his humanity. As a result his way becomes the way of simplicity, hard work, straightforwardness, humility and radical lack of control, the way of total dependence on the Father.

At the end of the temptations story, Luke introduces a new note: 'the devil left him to return at an opportune time.' Much later in his gospel Luke records what this 'opportune time' is – the time of the arrest of Jesus. 'This is your hour and the hour of the powers of darkness' (Luke 22:53).

The gospel stories of the temptations of Jesus are not minor stories about the devil tempting Jesus to commit sins. They are the radical temptations of embracing a false set of values opposed to Gospel values. We may be led more deeply into these Gospel values by contemplating Jesus at the end of the temptations. Having rejected the quick, slick, easy, controlling ways suggested by the devil, Jesus is left alone.

If we approach and ask him how he plans to make the kingdom come, perhaps his answer is something like this, 'I don't really know, but God's Spirit suggests to me that I should find good people and invite them to join me in spreading the message of God's love.' This, in fact, is what he did. With his disciples he began the slow, painstaking work of education that is still going on to this day, when, in fact, the kingdom is still coming.

— 20 —

Jesus Goes Home

When Jesus came to Nazareth, where he had been brought up, he went to the synagogue on the Sabbath day, as was his custom. He stood up to read, and the scroll of the prophet Isaiah was give to him. He unrolled the scroll and found the place where it was written, 'The Spirit of the Lord is upon me, because he has anointed me to bring good news to the poor. He has sent me to proclaim release to the captives and recovery of sight to the blind, to let the oppressed go free, to proclaim the year of the Lord's favour.'

And he rolled up the scroll, gave it back to the attendant and sat down. The eyes of all in the synagogue were fixed on him. Then he began to say to them, 'Today this scripture has been fulfilled in your hearing.'

All spoke well of him, and were amazed at the gracious words that came from his mouth. They said, 'Is not this Joseph's son?' He said to them, 'Doubtless you will quote me this proverb, "Doctor, cure yourself!" And you will say, "Do here also in your home town the things we have heard that you did at Capernaum."'

And he said, 'Truly I tell you, no prophet is accepted in the prophet's home town. But the truth is there were many widows in Israel in the time of Elijah when the heavens were shut up for three years and six months, and there was a severe famine over all the land; yet Elijah was sent to none of them except to the widow of Zarephath in Sidon. There were also many lepers in Israel in the time of the prophet Elisha, and none of them was cleansed except Naaman the Syrian.'

Jesus Goes Home

When they heard this, all in the synagogue were filled with rage. They got up, drove him out of the town, and led him to the brow of the hill on which their town was built, so that they might hurl him off the cliff. But he passed through the midst of them and went on his way.

Luke 4:16-30

IN MANY WAYS, this is one of the most striking passages in the gospels for our theme of contemplation and the Gospel. In the liturgy it is the gospel for Monday of the 22nd Week. It is also the gospel for the Chrism Mass on Holy Thursday.

The story of Jesus' return to Nazareth appears very early in the gospel of Luke. After two chapters of infancy narrative, he presents the baptism of Jesus and his genealogy; then the temptations, followed by our scene at Nazareth. Luke commences the passage by recording that Jesus went to the synagogue as was his Sabbath custom.

We may like to delay here with this striking insight into the humanness of Jesus. He is a Jew, and he brings to his public life all the values and limitations of his personal education: no sweeping changes to introduce a new religion! The focus on Jesus is a very visual one. 'He stood up to read.' Can I enter in my imagination into that image? I picture Jesus rising to his feet, and the attendant handing him the scroll of Isaiah and his unrolling of it.

Then, what a choice he makes. He claims as his own what Isaiah had presented as the mission of Israel. The gift of the Spirit and the anointing are the same words that are used by Peter in his sermon in the house of Cornelius: 'God anointed Jesus of Nazareth with the Holy Spirit and with power; and he went about doing good and healing all who were oppressed' (Acts 10:38). Isaiah's version of the mission which Jesus embraced is clearly, in our terminology, a preferential option for the poor. We may well delay to contemplate the symbolic meanings of the Isaiah passage, because each phrase encapsulates some aspect of the mission of every follower of Christ.

I too have been anointed with the Holy Spirit and with power. Who are 'the poor' in my life? What good news have I to bring them? Who are 'the captives'? How am I to set them free? What does it mean for me to bring new sight to 'the blind' and liberty to 'the oppressed'? How am I called to proclaim, in my living, my attitudes, my joy, that my God is indeed a God of favour?

Luke now reinforces the engagement of his readers' sense of sight in the handing back of the scroll to the attendant and Jesus

sitting down. He then drives it home with that wonderful line: 'The eyes of all in the synagogue were fixed on him.' Can I fix on him the eyes of my imagination? What do I see?

We have heard Jesus read. Now we hear him give the homily, in words that capture the purpose of every homily: 'Today this scripture has been fulfilled in your hearing.' How true this was of Jesus and these particular words of Isaiah! It is always the role of the homilist to relate the words of the readings to the real lives of the people who are present.

This is a truly contemplative experience, and when it happens one can sense the deep contemplative response of the hearers. Hopefully the homilist can sense that, like those in the synagogue with Jesus that day, those present 'wonder at the gracious words that come from his lips'.

What a wonderfully positive reaction the people present had, both visually and aurally, to Jesus among them – and how suddenly and dramatically it all changed! They displayed the typical fickleness of a crowd. Their spirit of contemplation suddenly changed into a carping, critical spirit about the local background of Jesus.

He, of course, had a ready reply. He knew them as a crowd whose deep-seated racism could not be suddenly overcome by a time of contemplatively looking and listening to him. The gift of contemplation always challenges us to allow it to penetrate those hidden areas of our hearts where our sinfulness may hold sway.

However, we cannot simply respond with thinking, 'What a crowd of racists those Nazarenes were.' Every one of us is challenged by the saying of Paul: 'There is neither Jew nor Greek, there is neither slave nor free, there is neither male nor female: for you are all one in Christ Jesus' (Galatians 3:28). Once again it may be necessary to focus our contemplation on this text, which so wonderfully directs us to an all-embracing love for all of God's people.

So incensed are the Nazarenes at Jesus for directing their attention to their racist tendencies that they try to kill him. For the time being his 'hour has not yet come', but it is this kind of confrontation that will lead eventually to his death and resurrection.

— 21 —

Happy the Poor in Spirit

When Jesus saw the crowds, he went up the mountain; and, after he sat down, his disciples came to him. Then he began to speak, and taught them, saying:

> 'Blessed are the poor in spirit, for theirs is the kingdom of heaven.
> Blessed are those who mourn, for they will be comforted.
> Blessed are the meek, for they will inherit the earth.
> Blessed are those who hunger and thirst for righteousness, for they will be filled.
> Blessed are the merciful, for they will receive mercy.
> Blessed are the pure in heart, for they will see God.
> Blessed are the peacemakers, for they will be called children of God.
> Blessed are those who are persecuted for righteousness' sake, for theirs is the kingdom of heaven.
> Blessed are you when people revile and persecute you and utter all kinds of evil against you falsely on my account. Rejoice and be glad, for your reward is great in heaven, for in the same way they persecuted the prophets who were before you.'
>
> Matthew 5:1-12

THE BEATITUDES OF MATTHEW are our gospel reading for the 4th Sunday of Year A, for Monday of the

Happy the Poor in Spirit

10th Week of Ordinary Time, and for the great solemnity of All Saints.

For the gospel of Matthew, Jesus is especially the great teacher. He is the new Moses. Moses went up the mountain to receive from God the Decalogue (the ten words of God), which laid the foundation for the Ten Commandments, and the Torah, the five books of the Law, the first five books of the Bible.

So Jesus goes up the mountain, not to receive but to proclaim nine Beatitudes, the charter of the new kingdom. We do well, of course, to begin our contemplation by focusing on Jesus, as he enters this solemn moment of his life under the loving gaze of the Father, Son and Holy Spirit. They gaze lovingly upon us too as we contemplate in their presence.

This is a truly happy occasion, and we may like to join in the picnic on the grassy slope, relaxed in the presence of Jesus and his disciples, before getting down to the serious business of the new law. Even when we do get down to business, we notice that this is a law with a difference. It does not come in the form, 'Thou shalt', and 'Thou shalt not', but rather, 'Happy are those who ...' The Beatitudes speak about those who experience God's blessings, and so are genuinely happy.

If there were nothing else, we should be eternally grateful for Matthew's first beatitude about the blessing of poverty of spirit. It situates us in our true perspective on life as human beings.

We are enfleshed spirits. We must live continuously with the paradox of being capable of the infinite, yet limited to the here and now. We are vulnerable in countless ways that we have never dreamed of. We are not in control of ourselves or of anybody else. At every instant we receive our being from Another. There is nothing we can do about it, except continue to receive it gratefully, living not by our own power, but by sheer gift. This is the positive side of the first beatitude. It is the defeat of the evil spirit who tried to persuade Adam and Eve that they could be like gods.

It is the same theme that will be spelt out by Matthew and Luke in their stories of the temptations of Jesus in the desert. One could go on at great length about the blessing of poverty of spirit. But it is not so much something to be understood, but something to be contemplated and lived contemplatively by putting into practice all the virtues of the Gospel itself.

Each of the Beatitudes spells out in its own way some aspect of the first one. The first beatitude proclaims that for those who embrace poverty of spirit 'theirs is the kingdom of heaven'. Later, Jesus proclaims the same blessing for those who are persecuted for the sake of justice. The reward of belonging to the kingdom of heaven is not so much to be seen as a reward after death by transfer to a better world. Rather it is the here and now existential blessing and happiness involved in 'right living'.

Some of the Beatitudes appear more paradoxical than others. What can be the comfort for those who are in mourning? Once again it is not a promise of comfort in the distant future, or when the mourning has passed. Rather it is the comfort here and now of having a right attitude in the face of grief, as well as other negative aspects of our human lives. By not striving to escape them or anaesthetize ourselves against them, we are being authentic human beings, knowing that the negative aspects of our lives must be gracefully accepted along with the positive.

How can it be true that the meek will inherit the earth? It is certainly not true if we think of 'inherit' as meaning acquire some kind of land title. What is true is that the meek are at home on planet Earth. They live in harmony with the Earth and all that is in it. They have a deep, contemplative respect for the environment. They do not exploit.

Particularly dear to St Ignatius of Loyola must have been the final beatitude. He expressed the high point of the contemplation of the mysteries of Christ in the *Spiritual Exercises* in what he called 'Three Degrees of Humility'. As he goes on to explain them, they turn out to be three degrees of being in love with Jesus.

A person who has gained the fruit of the contemplations on the mysteries of the life of Jesus will be so in love with him that they will desire to experience in their lives what he experienced. In order to be more like Jesus, they will have a preference for poverty, rejection and humiliation, rather than the opposites. This is a living out of the first beatitude to a heroic degree.

One would expect this degree of perfection of the spiritual life to be rather rare, but there people out there who really live it. Through our contemplations, may we at least grow to be more like them.

— 22 —

The Birds of the Air

Jesus said to his disciples, 'Therefore I tell you, do not worry about your life, what you will eat or what you will drink, or about your body, what you will wear. Is not life more than food, and the body more than clothing? Look at the birds of the air; they neither sow nor reap nor gather into barns, yet your heavenly Father feeds them. Are you not of more value than they?

'And can any of you, by worrying, add a single hour to your span of life? And why do you worry about clothing? Consider the lilies of the field, how they grow; they neither toil, nor spin, yet, I tell you, even Solomon in his glory was not clothed like one of these. But if God so clothes the grass of the field, which is alive today and tomorrow is thrown into the oven, will he not much more clothe you – you of little faith?

'Therefore do not worry, saying, "What will we eat?" or "What will we drink?" or "What will we wear?" For it is the Gentiles who strive for all these things; and indeed your heavenly Father knows that you need all these things. But strive first for the kingdom of God and his righteousness, and all things will be given to you as well.

'So do not worry about tomorrow, for tomorrow will bring worries of its own. Today's trouble is enough for today.'

Matthew 6:25-34

THIS IS THE GOSPEL for the 8th Sunday of Year A, as also for the Saturday of the 11th Week of Ordinary Time. The setting for our contemplation is again the mount of the Beatitudes. We make our preparatory prayer as usual, reminding ourselves of the Lord's presence, offering to him this time of prayer, and asking him that all our intentions, actions and operations may be directed only to his glory and the coming of his kingdom. We look into our hearts to find that deep desire for the grace we particularly want from the Lord, our God, at this time. We begin to name that grace in the context of our regular desire to know, love and follow Jesus better as an outcome of this time of contemplation.

We begin our prayer in contemplation of the Father, Son and Holy Spirit as they lovingly gaze upon Jesus in this early part of his mission to bring about the universal salvation of humankind. We too are a part of their plans and part of that mission through our priestly union with Jesus through baptism. Through our contemplation now may we better persons of prayer and action, ready to join more fully in the mission of Jesus. As we notice the large crowd of men, women and children who have gathered to listen to Jesus on the mountain, may we be aware of the persons in our own lives, those closest to us, and those whom we meet or just pass in the street this day. May we, even in the smallest way, be Christ on mission to all of them.

At first reading, it seems that this teaching of Matthew, and the corresponding teaching in Luke 12:22-34, are very different from the profound mysticism to be found in the writings of John or Paul. Yet, if we stop to give this teaching the attention it deserves in our contemplation, it can be every bit as rich and nourishing for the life of our spirit. The words are simple ones about very simple realities. They are words of homespun wisdom that could have come from the lips of any sage, prophet or guru. But as we read the gospel we are present to the Word of God in both senses of that term: first to the One who uttered them, and also to the Spirit-filled life that these images and messages impart. We look at and listen to Jesus more intently. We can say with Paul, 'For me to live is Christ' (Philippians 1:21), and with Peter, 'Lord to whom can we go? You have the words of eternal life' (John 6:68).

The call of Jesus to contemplate the birds of the air and the flowers of the field is an invitation to exercise that natural gift of contemplation which is God's gift to every person who comes into existence on this planet. The presence to mystery involved in such contemplation is not the sole preserve of Christians or religious people; it is for all. Whatever present phenomenon of creation we encounter, we can be present to the mystery of being, caught out of ourselves into true contemplation of any particular being – bird or flower, sunrise or sunset, bee or ant, no matter how big or small, no matter how near or far.

Wherever there is being, there is creation, and there also is the One who creates. Evil is always present to lure us back into ourselves, to the satisfaction of appetite or whim, to our thirst for possessions or honour or power, to inner states of worry or anxiety.

Our languages are full of expressions about the futility of worry. Many people are regularly worried because they find nothing to worry about, so have to turn to the two great certainties in their lives, death and taxes. Children, simple people and the truly poor are not anxious. They accept life and reality and all that they are called to be present to with a spirit of wonder, even of awe. We have only to watch children fascinated by a seagull while walking on the beach. They seem never to tire of the chase to catch it. They are caught out of themselves into the joy of the here and now presence to another in a game which they can never win. They are exercising the natural gift of contemplation.

We exercise the same natural gift of contemplation in encounters with other persons, especially those with whom we live, in a life-long relationship of marriage or of friendship, or even in a fleeting experiential moment of presence to someone we chance to meet. Genuine intimacy is clearly a gift of God.

Whenever we exercise this natural gift, if we are persons of faith, we are involved in contemplative prayer. The level of the prayer can be one of simple enjoyment of what we know, however vaguely, are God's gifts to us, all the way through to sublime mystical experience of the Creator. Every time we celebrate Eucharist we pray to be kept 'free from sin and from anxiety as we watch in joy and hope for the coming of our Saviour, Jesus Christ'.

Freedom from worry is not just a natural gift. It is that, but at the same time it is a gift of the Spirit to be received contemplatively in faith, hope and joy. People who choose to follow a life of contemplative prayer develop an inner spiritual strength that enables them to rise above situations in their lives that cause others to be filled with worry and anxiety. This is clearly the meaning of verse 33, 'strive first for the kingdom of God and his righteousness, and all these things will be given to you as well.' The Lord is not promising to endow us with 'things', but to gift us with poverty of spirit, a peace that enables us to be content no matter what the external situations in which we find ourselves.

Jesus concludes this section of the gospel with a masterstroke of wisdom, 'So do not worry about tomorrow, for tomorrow will bring worries of its own. Today's trouble is enough for today.' He invites us to live in the now, which is all that any of us has. The sacrament of the present moment is always God's gift to us, if we are contemplative enough to live it to the full.

— 23 —
Feeding of the Multitude

The apostles gathered around Jesus and told him all that they had done and taught. He said to them, 'Come away all by yourselves to a deserted place and rest a while.' For many were coming and going and they had no leisure even to eat. And they went away in the boat to a deserted place all by themselves. Now many saw them going and they recognized them and they hurried there on foot from all the towns and arrived there ahead of them.

As he went ashore, he saw a great crowd; and he had compassion for them because they were like sheep without a shepherd; and he began to teach them many things. When it grew late, his disciples came to him and said, 'This is a deserted place, and the hour is now very late; send them away so that they may go into the surrounding country and villages and buy something for themselves to eat.'

But he answered them, 'You give them something to eat.' They said to him, 'Are we to go and buy two hundred denarii worth of bread, and give it to them to eat?' And he said to them, 'How many loaves have you? Go and see.' When they had found out, they said, 'Five and two fish.' Then he ordered them to get all the people to sit down in groups on the green grass. So they sat down in groups of hundreds and of fifties.

Taking the five loaves and the fish, he looked up to heaven, and blessed and broke the loaves and gave them to the disciples to set before the people; and he divided the two fish among them all. And all ate and were filled; and

Feeding of the Multitude

they took up twelve baskets full of broken pieces and of the fish. Those who had eaten the loaves numbered five thousand men.

Mark 6:30-44

THE FIRST FOUR VERSES of this reading are the gospel for the 16th Sunday of Ordinary Time, Year B, and Saturday of the 4th week; the last eleven verses are the gospel for 8 January.

The gospel reading is the first of six accounts of the only miracle of Jesus that is recorded in all four gospels: the feeding of a multitude of people with a few loaves and fish. It appears twice in Mark (here and 8:1-10), and twice in Matthew (14:13-21 and 15,:32-39). Clearly it is of utmost importance in the Christian tradition. This is because of its very clear connection with the Eucharist. In the sequence of Mark's gospel it is followed by the great nature miracle of walking on water, as happens also in Matthew and John. Luke, who omits this, had already introduced (in 5:1-11) a great water miracle, the miraculous draft of fish, followed, as in the others, by a profession of faith on the part of Peter.

For Mark, the feeding of the 5000 introduces the great central section of his gospel which includes Peter's profession of faith in Jesus as the Messiah, the prophecies of the death and resurrection of Jesus, along with the disciples' failure to be contemplative enough to grasp those sayings, and the Transfiguration (Mark 8:14-21), immediately after the second feeding of the multitude, has a wonderful account of the attempt by Jesus to bring his disciples to contemplative awareness by asking them no fewer than nine challenging questions in the course of eight verses.

'Why are you talking about having no bread? Do you still

not perceive or understand? ... Are your hearts hardened? ... Do you have eyes and fail to see? ... Do you have ears and fail to hear?'... 'And do you not remember? When I broke the five loaves for the five thousand, how many baskets full of broken pieces did you collect?' They said to him, 'Twelve.' 'And the seven for the four thousand, how many baskets full of broken pieces did you collect?' And they said to him, 'Seven.' Then he said to them, 'Do you not yet understand?'

All of this can be summarized in one question: 'Are you not yet contemplative enough?' The same reality is referred to by John after his account of the feeding of the 5000 in the words of Jesus: 'Very truly, I tell you, you are looking for me, not because you saw signs, but because you ate your fill of the loaves. Do not work for the food that perishes, but for the food that endures for eternal life' (John 6:26-27)

The context of the feeding miracle for Mark is a presentation of the very intimate relationship of Jesus and the disciples. I may well enter in my contemplation into this relationship. As I reflect on myself, I too may be aware of how demanding are life itself and importunate people for me. I look at Jesus and his reactions. I reflect that as Lord he is always with me and always in control even of what is most demanding in my life. I may well enter into conversation with him about this.

I look too at his disciples, perhaps share their anxiety, and may also want to converse with them, especially with my friends or patrons among them. He invites them to come away for a time of rest and quiet after their very laborious and successful time of mission among very demanding groups of people.

Jesus begins to display a lightness of touch in the relationship, along with a sense of humour. He seems to know well that for the disciples things are to get even more hectic. No sooner had they reached their deserted place of retreat than a vast crowd began to appear. This threw his disciples into something of a state of panic. Jesus by contrast is totally calm and full of compassion for the crowd, seeming to know well what will happen. So he continues the mission, teaching them many things.

Jesus doesn't seem to notice the time slipping by, but the disciples do! They come to him and express their anxiety: 'Send them away, so that can get something to eat.' This evokes a humorous response from Jesus: 'Give them something to eat yourselves.' But they are still serious. In modern terms it would cost about $60,000 to feed them – 5000 people at $12 a head; just about right. Jesus continues to pull their legs: 'How many loaves have you?' Mark alone then has the people divide into groups of about fifty or a hundred and sit down on the green grass. This is the kind of simple, graphic, eyewitness-type detail characteristic of his style and perhaps a help to our contemplation and sense of presence.

Now we have the point of the whole story: Jesus took the five loaves and the two fish, blessed (meaning thanked the Father, from which we get the word 'Eucharist'), broke the loaves, and gave them to the disciples to set before the people.

This same Eucharistic formula, already in use in the early church at the time of writing, is common to all six accounts of the feeding of the multitude. The same words are used in our Eucharist to this day. The various accounts treat the question of the fish differently. In almost all of them, the fish have a secondary part – they hardly belong at the heart of the Christian Eucharist! Whenever we approach the Eucharist we need to come with that contemplative attitude that has been so characteristic of God's people throughout the ages, and which these pages are meant to foster.

Because this contemplation is focused so clearly on the Eucharist, I may do well to turn to Father, Son and Holy Spirit to pray for a deeper appreciation of what Eucharist means to me, and of the part each of the Divine Persons plays in it. It is a very important prayer; so I can be helped in it by approaching Mary and Jesus, the two great intercessors, and asking each of them to help me in my relationship with the Trinity.

— 24 —

Who Do You Say I Am?

Jesus went on with his disciples to the villages of Caesarea Philippi; and on the way he asked his disciples, 'Who do people say that I am?' And they answered him, 'John the Baptist; and others, Elijah; and still others one of the prophets.' He asked them, 'But who do you say that I am?' Peter answered him, 'You are the Messiah.' And he sternly ordered them not to tell anyone about him.

Then he began to teach them that the Son of Man must undergo great suffering, and be rejected by the chief priests, the elders and the scribes, and be killed, and after three days rise again. He said all this quite openly. And Peter took him aside and began to rebuke him. But turning and looking at his disciples, he rebuked Peter and said, 'Get behind me, Satan, because you are setting your mind not on divine things but on human things.' He called the crowd together with his disciples, and said to them, 'If any want to become my followers, let them deny themselves and take up their cross and follow me. For those who want to save their life will lose it, and those who lose their life for my sake and for the sake of the gospel will save it.'

Mark 8:27-35

THIS IS OUR GOSPEL READING for the 24th Sunday of Ordinary Time, Year B, a most important gospel passage, and one that is rich indeed for our contemplation.

We begin our time of prayer, as always, by recalling the

presence of the Lord whom we contemplate and offering to him the time we have chosen to give to this exercise. I then compose myself for prayer by allowing my imagination to focus on the historical, geographical setting for this mystery. Jesus has spent half of his public ministry in teaching and healing in order to bring his disciples to that personal relationship with him which we call 'faith'. He has been moving around his home province of Galilee, and now has gone further north away from the sea of Galilee to the region around Caesarea Philippi. And it is here in a more foreign setting that he will ask for this vital profession of faith in him.

We are about to enter upon the centrepiece of the whole gospel. I begin to pray for the grace I desire. As always in contemplating a mystery of the gospels, it is to have a deeper personal knowledge of Jesus, to love him more deeply and to follow him more closely in living my life.

I begin my contemplation slowly and carefully; first by seeing the persons involved in the mystery. The first Persons to be considered are God: Father, Son and Holy Spirit, who are always present to Jesus, as he carries out his mission of universal salvation. The same trinitarian persons are right now present to me as I endeavour to be one with the risen Lord in carrying out my personal mission of continuing his work of salvation.

I turn my attention next to contemplate the person of Jesus. I see him in my imagination; perhaps the image is not very clear, but the essence of this exercise is that I am now more deeply present to him, who is my Life and my Salvation.

I see in my mind's eye the other persons: Peter, with whom I probably already have a real personal relationship; the other disciples, some of them perhaps personal favourites of mine; the vastly diverse members of the crowd – some curious, some

Who Do You Say I Am?

sceptical, some interested, some full of despair about their lives, others full of hope and longing. Where do I stand among this motley group?

Next I allow myself to see what each of these persons is doing in the gospel story of the mystery – Jesus teaching, the disciples wondering and striving to listen, the members of the crowd each with their own personal reaction. And what about me? How am I ready to participate as the story unfolds?

Now I turn to what I have perhaps been waiting for: to hear what each one says. But it is only by going slowly through each of the foregoing steps that I am truly ready to hear at depth. Clearly, the initial question of Jesus – 'Who do you say I am?' – was not looking for an intellectual discourse but for an expression of interpersonal relationship.

In their uncertainty about the afterlife, the Jews responded in typical fashion, seeing Jesus as a great man in the spirit of their past heroes. Rightly Jesus ignores this reincarnationism, and very firmly puts the question again: 'But, you, who do you say I am?' Peter, obviously assuming a leadership role, speaks up. 'You are the Messiah.' The Greek word is 'Christ', the Hebrew 'Messiah'. Later Matthew will embellish this simple Petrine affirmation by adding the Christian formula, 'the Son of the living God'.

Each praying person must respond to the great question in their own way, be it in one or more words, or by simply resting in the presence of the Lord Jesus in silence. I might like to delay at this point for some time, allowing him to nourish in me that faith that is essential for a disciple.

The simple profession of initial faith by Peter now inspires Jesus to begin the radically new teaching about discipleship, the following of him by the way of the cross, that will dominate the rest of the gospel. Immediately Peter misunderstands, even rejects, this teaching. Jesus makes it clear to him that to think in the manner of fallen humanity, unenlightened by the Spirit, is to be on the side of Satan.

From now on Jesus will have to repeat often his instruction about true discipleship being via the way of the cross. It will only be through the post-Resurrection outpouring of the Holy Spirit that they finally grasp his full message. Each of us, rejoicing in the gift of that same Holy Spirit, has the opportunity to grasp it now. We are called to appreciate Jesus who is the Way (John 14:6) by taking to heart in contemplation the great saying of Jesus, recorded six times in the course of the four gospels: 'Anyone who wants to save their life will lose it; but anyone who loses their life for my sake, and for the sake of the Gospel, will save it.'

As Jesus asks me for my profession of personal faith in him, I cannot rush into a 'top of the head' answer. I have to look deep within myself, to be very truthful about something I may scarcely be able to put into words. I turn to Mary. She is vitally interested in my answer. I ask her: 'Who was Jesus for you?' I listen carefully to her response. I turn to Jesus and ask him really to reveal himself to me.

In their presence I make the same prayer to Father, to Son, and to Holy Spirit. I listen to each. I turn back to Jesus, and hopefully can now respond to him with what has just now been revealed to me.

— 25 —

You are the Messiah

When Jesus came into the district of Caesarea Philippi, he asked his disciples, 'Who do you say that the Son of Man is?' And they said, 'Some say John the Baptist, but others Elijah, and still others Jeremiah or one of the prophets.' He said to them, 'But who do you say that I am?' Simon Peter answered, "You are the Messiah, the Son of the living God.'

And Jesus answered him, 'Blessed are you Simon, son of Jonah! For flesh and blood has not revealed this to you, but my Father in heaven. And I tell you, you are Peter, and on this rock I will build my church, and the gates of Hades will not prevail against it. I will give you the keys of the kingdom of heaven, and whatever you bind on earth will be bound in heaven, and whatever you loose on earth will be loosed in heaven.'

Matthew 16:13-19.

THIS IS THE GOSPEL READING for the 21st Sunday of Ordinary Time. It is a text which, in a variety of forms, is central to each of the four gospels.

I may compose myself for contemplation of this mystery of the Lord by focusing via my imagination on the setting: the gathering of Jesus and his disciples in Galilee by the lake (John), or further north at Caesarea Philippi (Mark, Matthew). Following the way of St Ignatius, I begin to ask for whatever grace I now desire. It may well be a deepening of my faith-relationship with the Lord Jesus by getting in touch with what he really means for me in my life.

In our 'divine reading' of the text, we may note the habit of the Jewish people of identifying any great present person with one of the greats of the past: St John the Baptist, Elijah, Jeremiah, or another of the prophets. This is clearly background for the real issue the gospel text is raising, namely, who is Jesus for a Christian disciple? Who is Jesus for Peter? Who is Jesus for me?

Not only does it give us immediate matter for our personal contemplation and a challenge for each of us, but it is very instructive for our understanding of the different stances of each of the four gospel writers. Matthew gives us the most fully developed of the four, so it is the one that most people remember. Not only that. The idea of Peter holding 'the keys of the kingdom of heaven' has passed into popular folklore through innumerable jokes about meeting him at the 'pearly gates'.

In Mark, Peter's reply is, 'You are the Holy One of God.' Any attempt to recapture historically what Peter may have actually said is futile, and is a distraction in prayer. If I must ask, it is probably best to settle for Mark, the first of the four gospels: 'You are the Messiah.' This is the simplest, least theologically embellished, and Mark is generally considered to be closest to an eyewitness account.

Whatever about this distraction, the purpose of each of the gospels is not historicity, as we understand that word, but gospel truth, which enriches our minds and hearts and the whole of our life in the Spirit. Matthew's text is clearly a later theological development of Mark. 'You are the Messiah, the Son of the loving God' is a beautiful expression of the living truth of who Jesus is for all Christian people. We may well choose to remain here in contemplation of this profound truth.

You Are the Messiah

In his first book of spiritual stories, *The Song of the Bird*, Tony de Mello gives us this striking reflection of Peter's profession of faith. Jesus asks his disciples, 'Who do you say I am?' Peter replies, 'You are the Son of the Living God.' Jesus then praises Peter because 'Flesh and blood has not revealed this to you, but my Father in heaven.' Jesus then asks me the same question, and I reply, 'You are the Son of the Living God.' To which Jesus responds, 'Right. But how unfortunate you are that you have learnt this only from others. It has not yet been revealed to you by my Father.'

While my repetition of Peter's words of faith may be a richly authentic expression of the fruit of this contemplation for me, there is always the danger of staying at the level of a verbal theological formula instead of going deeper into a contemplatively experienced reality.

A very good case to the point is the story of Martha in John's account of the raising of Lazarus. When Jesus invites her to express her faith, she replies, 'Lord, I believe that you are the Christ, the Son of God, who has come into the world.' This is a very good 'catechism' answer. A moment later Jesus invites Martha to a real, practical expression of faith: 'Take away the stone.' This is too much for Martha, and she protests, which leads Jesus to rebuke her, 'Did I not tell you that if you believed, you would see the glory of God?'

Clearly, I must not fixate on the question 'Who do you say that I am?' as one addressed only to the disciples present in the historical setting. It is a key question for every Christian disciple today. As I contemplate, I know that it is addressed to me personally. Clearly, too, the question does not seek a catechism answer, but I must search my heart in prayer to get in touch with what my relationship with Jesus means to me here and now in my life.

Each relationship is unique. Each response to the question

must be unique. A verbal reply can be an obstacle. There is a reality here that is truly ineffable, that is, beyond all words. Equally a verbal reply can be really authentic. Each of us in the depth of our personal prayer responds with a living faith which will show forth its fruit in the way that we live the Gospel.

— 26 —

Jesus Is Transfigured

Six days later, Jesus took with him Peter and James and his brother John and led them up a high mountain, by themselves. And he was transfigured before them and his face shone like the sun, and his clothes became dazzling white. Suddenly there appeared to them Moses and Elijah talking with him. Then Peter said to Jesus, 'Lord, it is good for us to be here; if you wish, I will make three dwellings here, one for you, one for Moses, and one for Elijah.'

While he was still speaking, suddenly a bright cloud overshadowed them, and from the cloud a voice said, 'This is my Son, the Beloved; with him I am well pleased; listen to him!'

When the disciples heard this, they fell to the ground and were overcome by fear. But Jesus came and touched them, saying, 'Get up and do not be afraid.' And when they looked up, they saw no one except Jesus himself alone.

Matthew 17:1-8

THE 2ND SUNDAY OF LENT is Transfiguration Sunday. In Year A, as on the Feast of the Transfiguration, Year A, the gospel reading is from Matthew.

When Pope John Paul II proclaimed the fourth set of mysteries of the Rosary, the Mysteries of Light, he faced the difficulty of choosing just five from all the mysteries of the public life of Jesus. It was no accident that great prominence was given to the twin mysteries, the Baptism in the Jordan (first mystery) and the Transfiguration (fourth mystery).

The Baptism is the proclamation of the Father, anointing Jesus with power for the carrying out of his ministry; the Transfiguration is, so to speak, the repetition of the Baptism proclamation with respect to the coming suffering, death and resurrection of Jesus. The principal difference is that, in the Baptism scene, the words of love and affirmation of Jesus are addressed to him personally, as is emphasized in the gospels of Mark and Luke. The Transfiguration proclamation, on the other hand, is addressed to the three chosen disciples, Peter, James and John, the same three who will accompany Jesus in Gethsemane.

It is helpful to reflect that in the gospel of John, which does not narrate the Transfiguration story directly, there is an oblique reference to this mystery in John 12: 28-30. When the voice of the Father is heard, Jesus declares to the crowd, 'This voice has come for your sake, not for mine.'

The role of the Transfiguration is to prepare the disciples for the coming scandal of the cross by a foretaste of the glory of the Lord's resurrection. This is why the church gives us this mystery for our contemplation on the second Sunday of Lent each year. In Year A, we take our contemplation from the gospel of Matthew, in the following years from Mark and Luke.

It is always helpful to reflect on the differences of text in the three synoptic gospels. Matthew, with his interest in family and personal relationship, is the only one to refer here to John as the brother of James. He alone emphasizes the glory of Jesus with the words 'his face shone like the sun'. Only Matthew mentions the brightness of the cloud that overshadowed the disciples. The mention of the cloud is a clear reference to the glory of the Lord that accompanied Israel in its desert pilgrimage (Exodus 16:10, 24:15-18).

When Peter speaks to Jesus ('Lord, it is good for us to be here'), out of respect for Peter, the leader of the disciples,

Jesus Is Transfigured

Matthew omits the words of Mark which Luke also included: 'He did not know what he was talking about.' It is only in Matthew that the words of the Father cause great fear in the disciples. This leads to the reassurance of Jesus in his often repeated words, 'Do not be afraid', accompanied here by the Lord's gentle and encouraging touch.

Matthew emphasizes the final state of the disciples in finding the presence of Jesus in all that they need with the words, '... they saw no one except Jesus himself alone.'

The mystery of the Lord's death and resurrection, like all his mysteries, is firmly grounded in the Old Testament. This is why all the Transfiguration accounts tell of the appearance of the two towering Old Testament figures – Moses, representing the Torah, the books of the Law, and Elijah, representing the Prophets. We are being invited to contemplate the great continuity of Salvation History, and to deepen our awareness of the rich Old Testament background that will influence the gospel accounts of our Lord's suffering and death, and will therefore figure prominently in the readings of the coming Lent.

Outstanding among these Old Testament references are the four great 'servant songs' of the prophet Isaiah. So the words of the Father addressed to the disciples in the Transfiguration are the opening words of the first song of the suffering servant, 'Here is my servant, whom I uphold, my chosen, in whom my soul delights.' Only Matthew gives us the fullest interpretation of this text in the words spoken by the Father, 'This is my Son, the Beloved; with him I am well pleased; listen to him!'

All three, Matthew, Mark and Luke, conclude with the words, 'Listen to him!' This sounds like an excellent exhortation for the best way to spend our times of contemplation in the coming Lent! As always, we must remember that this whole scene is enacted in the presence of Father, Son and Holy Spirit with whom we are always welcome to have conversation.

— 27 —

Lose Your Life

Jesus began to teach them that the Son of Man must undergo great suffering, and be rejected by the elders, the chief priests and the scribes, and be killed, and after three days rise again. He said all of this quite openly. And Peter took him aside and began to rebuke him. But turning and looking at his disciples, Jesus rebuked Peter and said, 'Get behind me, Satan! For you are setting your mind not on divine things, but on human things.'

Jesus called the crowd with his disciples, and said to them, 'If any want to become my followers, let them deny themselves and take up their cross and follow me. For those who want to save their life will lose it, and those who lose their life for my sake, and the sake of the gospel, will save it. For what will it profit them to gain the whole world and forfeit their life?'

Mark, 8:31-36

Then they came to Capernaum; and when he was in the house, he asked them, 'What were you arguing about on the way?' But they were silent, because on the way they had argued with one another who was the greatest. He sat down, called the twelve and said to them, 'Whoever wants to be the first must be the last of all and servant of all.' Then he took a little child and put it among them; and taking it in his arms, he said to them, 'Whoever welcomes one such child in my name welcomes me, and whoever welcomes me welcomes not me but the one who sent me.'

Mark 9:33-37

Lose Your Life

THE FIRST OF THESE READINGS is taken from the gospel for the 24th Sunday of Ordinary Time, Year B. The second is from the gospel for the 25th Sunday of Ordinary Time, Year C, and also from Tuesday of the 7th Week of Ordinary Time.

After making our usual preparatory prayer, offering all our intentions, actions and operations to the Lord, we focus our attention on Jesus, on the disciples, and on the little child in their midst. We begin to pray that we will better know, love and follow him in taking to heart his fundamental word of losing our life in order to find it. This will involve me more and more in going out of myself to be on mission to all to whom I am sent. These are primarily the people with whom I live, and also those who are poor, in all the varied dimensions of human poverty.

In Mark's gospel, immediately after Peter's initial profession of faith, 'You are the Messiah' (Mark 8:29), Jesus begins his prophecies of his coming Passion. He repeats these in chapters 9 and 10. They can only be accepted by those who are contemplative enough to do so, and the disciples are not. As Jesus says to Peter after the first time, 'You are setting your mind not on divine things, but on human things.'

The disciples' lack of response is underlined by their continually entering into argument about who will be the greatest in the kingdom. Clearly they set their minds on an earthly kingdom of power and prestige. Everyone who wants to belong to Christ's kingdom must have the opposite mindset.

As we enter on the contemplation of this mystery, we are called to pray that we will be contemplative enough to understand, not only in our minds but in our hearts, to have a growing commitment to embracing the way of Jesus, because we love him who is the Way.

Immediately after the first prophecy of his suffering, death and resurrection, Jesus calls us all to take up our particular cross and follow him and explains this with the only saying of his that appears in all four gospels: 'Those who try to save their life will lose it, and those who lose their life for my sake, and for the sake of the gospel, will save it.' Not only is this saying in each of the four gospels, but it appears twice in Matthew (after the first prophecy of the Passion, and again in Matthew 10:39), and twice in Luke (after the first prophecy of the Passion, and again in Luke 17:33).

This great saying of Jesus is not only at the heart of all authentic Christian spirituality, it is also the fundamental law of nature. Wherever we look in the plant or animal kingdoms, it is fulfilled. All of them, like us, are 'born to die'. Life cannot be protected and hoarded; it must be handed on and given away if a creature is to have the experience of being truly alive.

Life is for living. To live is to be insecure and vulnerable, and really to live is to embrace our insecurity and vulnerability; it is to embrace the first beatitude: 'Happy are the poor in spirit.'

In Paris, Ignatius of Loyola met a fellow student named Francis Xavier, like Ignatius a Basque from northern Spain. Ignatius knew Francis as a most talented person, a brilliant student, and a fine athlete as well. Ignatius saw in him a latent capacity for good. Francis was very keen to make the *Spiritual Exercises*, the book Ignatius had been working on for ten years since his conversion. Along with the talents Ignatius saw in Francis, he discerned a powerful ambition to be a successful man of the world. He wanted to be 'the greatest'.

It took some years before Ignatius judged Francis ready for the *Spiritual Exercises*. It is said that during this time Ignatius endlessly repeated to Francis, 'What would it profit to gain the whole world and forfeit your own life?' With the grace of God Francis Xavier opened his heart to the essence of the Gospel message.

The struggle between the sayings of Jesus and his disciples' desire to be the greatest continues throughout chapters 8, 9 and 10 of Mark's gospel. Luke even notices the same phenomenon at the institution of the Eucharist! The words of institution are in 22:19-20. In verse 24, 'A dispute arose among them as to which of them was to be regarded as the greatest.'

What a contrast between on the one hand, 'my body given for you and my blood poured out for you', and on the other, 'wanting to be the greatest'. It is the conflict in which every one of us is engaged. The only way to victory is to contemplate the example and words of Jesus, and to pray earnestly for God's grace.

In our second reading, Jesus proposes to the disciples the example of the small child. The main characteristics of small children are innocence and simplicity and total dependence upon their parents and other adults for absolutely everything. For them poverty of spirit is not a choice; it is an absolute necessity. Jesus took a small child, put it in the midst of the disciples and took it in his arms to teach by prophetic actions that his way is the way of weakness, vulnerability and self-emptying.

What a scene for our contemplation! Jesus, the child in his arms, the embarrassment of the disciples, confronted with this image in the very act of wanting to be number one. Later, Jesus will sum up his teaching in the famous words: 'The Son of Man came not to be served, but to serve, and to give his life as a ransom for many' (Mark: 10:45). The idea of Christian service has nothing to do with an 'upstairs-downstairs' mentality. It is simply a willingness to carry out our mission by assisting in whatever way we can those God sends our way in need of our love.

Because we are dealing here with our response to the great saying of Jesus which is the heart of the Gospel, we may do especially well in asking Mary to intercede for us, praying to Jesus for the grace of that same response, and asking them to lead us to the Divine Persons to receive that grace.

— 28 —

Preparing for the Passion

Now among those who went up to worship at the festival were some Greeks. They came to Philip, who was from Bethsaida in Galilee, and said to him, 'Sir, we wish to see Jesus.' Philip went and told Andrew; then Andrew and Philip went and told Jesus.

    Jesus answered them, 'The hour has come for the Son of Man to be glorified. Very truly I tell you, unless a grain of wheat falls into the earth and dies, it remains just a single grain; but if it dies, it bears much fruit. Those who love their life lose it, and those who hate their life in this world will keep it for eternal life. Whoever serves me must follow me, and where I am there will my servant be also. Whoever serves me, the Father will honour. Now my soul is troubled. And what should I say? Father, save me out of this hour. It is for this reason that I have come to this hour. Father, glorify your name.'

    Then a voice came from heaven, 'I have glorified it, and I will glorify it again.' The crowd standing there heard it and said it was thunder. Others said, 'An angel has spoken to him.' Jesus answered, 'This voice has come for your sake, not for mine.'

John 12:20-30

THIS IS THE GOSPEL for the 5th Sunday of Lent, Year B.

In this remarkable passage, the evangelist John brings together a whole cluster of different Scripture texts of

Preparing for the Passion

preparation for the coming sufferings and death of Jesus which the other three evangelists treat in more detail and in a much more spread out way.

We go through our usual steps for entering into contemplation. We pray in every mystery to know, love and follow Jesus, our Lord. We begin always in the presence of Father, Son and Holy Spirit, as they gaze upon Jesus, and upon me, filled with love. For our contemplation we ponder these most significant sayings of Jesus.

The passage starts with a request from some Greek visitors to Jerusalem for an introduction to Jesus: 'Sir, we wish to see Jesus.' The word 'see', as so many Johannine words do, has a double meaning. It has the ordinary meaning of the word, but it is also one of John's words for 'believe into', as are the words 'come to'. This leads Jesus to reflect that the gift of faith will only be possible as an outcome of his suffering, death and glorification. For John this is the hour of glorification; so Jesus opens his reflection with a clear statement of this: 'The hour has come for the Son of Man to be glorified.'

Jesus now goes on to spell out what will lead to his glorification, along with the necessary conditions of discipleship, something which Mark spreads out in chapters 8, 9 and 10 of his gospel. And John starts this with a very striking one verse parable which is unique to his gospel, the very powerful image of the death of the grain of wheat to produce 'much fruit'. This image has become a great favourite as an image of discipleship through death-resurrection. It could be most helpful to sit in contemplation with this particular image.

Then follows the radical statement which is the only saying of Jesus found in all four gospels: 'Those who love their life will lose it; those who hate their life in this world will keep it for eternal life.' He goes on to point out that this general, all-pervading principle applies especially to anyone who wants to be a disciple: 'If anyone serves me, they must follow me, and where I am there shall my servant be also.' This leads to a share in the glorification: 'If anyone serves me, the Father will honour them.'

Now we have a dramatic shift of focus to the prayer of Jesus in Gethsemane, as John cites the same words that appear in that context in Mark and Matthew: 'Now is my soul troubled.' John continues with the Gethsemane theme. 'What should I say? Father, save me out of this hour.' The translation 'out of' is correct; the more usual 'from' is not. The prayer of Jesus before his Passion is not a plea to be saved from dying, but a prayer to be saved out of death (as in Hebrews 5:7). This is what in fact did take place in the Resurrection. The correct translation also makes the statement of Jesus a real one, rather than a strange hypothetical: 'What should I say? – No, I won't say that.'

John concludes this account of the prayer of Jesus with the words: 'Father, glorify your name.' This will be his repeated prayer to the Father in the great prayer of chapter 17, John's version of Matthew's and Luke's Lord's Prayer. John's phrase is a clear equivalent of their 'Father, hallowed be thy name.'

For John, the 'hour' of Jesus (verse 23 above) is the hour of his glorification, or the hour 'to depart out of this world to the Father' (John 13:1). This prayer of Jesus now receives an immediate answer. A voice is heard from heaven declaring, 'I have glorified it, and I will glorify it again.' The Father has glorified his name through the signs that Jesus has worked throughout the gospel of John, and now will definitively glorify his name in the death-resurrection of Jesus.

In each of the three synoptic gospels the voice from heaven is heard at the Baptism of Jesus and again at the Transfiguration, six times in all. This is the only time it appears in John. In Mark, Matthew and Luke the Transfiguration is linked to prophecies of Jesus about his coming Passion and his statements about the conditions of discipleship.

Moreover, just as at the Transfiguration the voice spoke to the three disciples, Peter, James and John – 'This is my beloved Son. Listen to him' – so here Jesus declares to the crowd around: 'This voice came for your sake, not for mine.' The conclusion is that for John this episode is a clear reference to the Lord's Transfiguration.

Our passage from John 12 is indeed a rich one for our contemplation. It leads us into our relationship with the Father through the prayer of Jesus. Don't neglect to converse with each of them. It gives us the powerful image of dying and rising in the grain of wheat image. We are drawn to contemplate the greatest saying of the gospels, the only words of Jesus to be quoted by all four: about losing our life to find it. Then comes a powerful statement of the union with Jesus involved in discipleship. We go to Gethsemane and join in the Lord's Prayer.

Finally John shows that he is no stranger to the Transfiguration. Jesus will be glorified; and we will follow him in his way and so be honoured by the Father. Don't neglect to converse with Father, Son and Holy Spirit about this invitation to follow Jesus all the way by living out our baptism.

— 29 —
Gethsemane

Then Jesus said to them, 'You will all become deserters because of me this night; for it is written, "I will strike the shepherd, and the sheep of the flock will be scattered."'

Then Jesus went with them to a place called Gethsemane, and he said to his disciples, 'Sit here while I go over there and pray.' He took with him Peter and the two sons of Zebedee, and began to be grieved and agitated. Then he said to them, 'I am deeply grieved, even to death; remain here, and stay awake with me.' And, going a little further, he threw himself on the ground and prayed, 'My Father, if it is possible, let this cup pass from me; yet not what I want but what you want.'

Then he came to the disciples and found them sleeping; and he said to Peter, 'So, could you not stay awake with me one hour? Stay awake and pray that you may not come into the time of trial; the spirit indeed is willing but the flesh is weak.' Again he went away for the second time and prayed, 'My Father, if this cannot pass unless I drink it, your will be done.'

Again he came and found them sleeping, for their eyes were heavy. So leaving them again, he went away and prayed again, saying the same words. Then he came to the disciples and said to them, 'Are you still sleeping and taking your rest? See, the hour is at hand, and the Son of Man is betrayed into the hands of sinners. Get up, let us be going. See, my betrayer is at hand.'

Matthew 26:31; 36-46

Gethsemane

IN THE LITURGY, the prayer of Jesus in Gethsemane is part of Matthew's Passion account, which is read on Passion (Palm) Sunday, Year A.

Given the solemnity of our joining Jesus in prayer at this fundamental moment in the history of the human race up till now, it seems important that we should go through our usual preparation for prayer particularly slowly and thoughtfully.

The scene is not difficult to imagine. Jesus and his eleven disciples have just crossed the small valley of Kedron alongside Jerusalem, and gone a short distance up the initial slope of Mt Olivet. There they reach a small space among the many olive trees, and Jesus enters upon his prayer. Do I really want to know, love and follow him? If so, I begin my prayer by asking for that grace. With what love the Father, Son and Holy Spirit look upon Jesus as he moves into this crucial time of prayer.

We enter into contemplation of the greatest prayer ever prayed, the prayer of Jesus on the threshold of his separation from his disciples in death. It is important to cite verse 31 above about the scattering of the sheep, as it gives the very significant context of the Gethsemane prayer. The same context is given by John when, at the end of chapter 16, he writes about the scattering of the disciples. Again this is immediately before the prayer of Jesus (John 17), which is immediately before his arrest (John 18:1).

The prayer of Jesus is the same in Mark, Matthew, Luke and John. In all four it is fundamentally the same as the Lord's Prayer, given in Luke chapter 11 and in Matthew chapter 6. So, for Mark, Matthew and John, Jesus goes to his prayer preoccupied about the imminent scattering of the disciples, not just about his own approaching death. Luke is different; he does not acknowledge the scattering of the disciples; after all, they are the pillars of the church!

Plenty of people have accepted death courageously. Do we

expect Jesus to be any less courageous? In none of the gospels is it mentioned that Jesus has a fear of dying. That is not what causes him to be in the extreme state of shock and terror which Mark wrote of as Jesus entered Gethsemane. It is clear that Jesus will now die. It is also clear to him that the disciples will give up, and, seemingly, the kingdom will not come. That is what causes Jesus to suffer the most extraordinary distress – understandably!

Both Mark and Matthew mention that Jesus prayed three times. This can be a convention for meaning he prayed long and earnestly, as Paul did in his account of his prayer experience in 2 Corinthians 12:8. It is interesting to notice that, although Paul's experience is so different from that of Jesus in Gethsemane, each of them receives multiple answers to their prayer which in neither case included the answer they started out seeking.

What we are specially indebted to Matthew for among all the gospel passages of the Gethsemane prayer is that he is the only one who takes us through the process of development in the prayer of Jesus. Matthew presents three stages in the prayer:

1. 'My Father, if it is possible, let this cup pass from me; yet, not my will, but yours be done.'
2. 'My Father, if this cannot pass unless I drink it, your will be done.'
3. 'Your will be done.'

In his prayer, Jesus enters a double dialogue: first, one-to-one with the Father; second, with the events going on around him in the matter about which he is praying. That matter is the plight of the disciples who, in this most crucial moment in the history of the human race, are giving up. Jesus had exhorted them to pray not to succumb to the great trial of the enemy, and they simply give up. This is what their sleep symbolizes.

In the instruction, 'watch with me' the two little words

'with me' definitely do not signify that Jesus is looking for support from the disciples. The opposite is true; he is praying in support of them. After finding them asleep he knows that it is not possible for the cup (the negative side of his dying) to pass, so he drops these words in the second prayer.

When Matthew wrote that Jesus prayed a third time, saying the same words, he was surely indicating the prayer of Jesus was going to a new depth. 'The same words' were the last words of the previous prayer, 'Your will be done.' These words indicate the total acceptance of what is happening.

As a result, we can see multiple answers to the prayer of Jesus in Gethsemane:

1. Jesus moves from a state of great distress to one of clear, deep peace.
2. He hears the Father say, 'Trust me; leave it to me.'
3. The disciples will receive the gift of the Holy Spirit and go forth on mission – after the Resurrection.
4. The kingdom will come, and is coming right now.

Contemplation is always a listening, at progressively more profound depth, to what the Father is revealing to us. Commenting on the Gethsemane prayer of Jesus, the author of the Letter to the Hebrews wrote: 'Although he was Son, Jesus learned obedience through what he suffered' (Hebrews 5:8).

Entering Gethsemane Jesus could not simply say, 'I always do the will of the One who sent me, so your will be done.' He had to come to terms with his disciples' giving up. 'Through what he suffered' means going through the twofold human process of observing what was happening and taking it to the Father in prayer.

Obedience, in the letter to the Hebrews, literally means 'hearing at depth'. Here we see just a few of the multiple answers to the prayer of Jesus in Gethsemane. Through our contemplation may we be led to see more deeply into the prayer of Jesus, and so pray more deeply ourselves.

Let us turn in our prayer to Mary. She was spared actual physical presence at the scene in Gethsemane, but knew all the pain of a mother's heart as her Son approached his last hours of dreadful suffering. We speak to her about what she experienced, and gradually ask her to take us into the presence of her Son. Perhaps we tell her of our wonder at the depth of his love for the disciples and for us.

Will Mary and Jesus accompany us as we come into the presence of the Trinity, as we speak to each one about what is in our hearts?

— 30 —

He Is Risen

The two disciples told what had happened on the road, and how he had been made known to them in the breaking of the bread.

While they were talking about this, Jesus himself stood among them and said to them, 'Peace be with you.' They were startled and terrified, and thought that they were seeing a ghost. He said to them, 'Why are you frightened, and why do doubts arise in your hearts? Look at my hands and my feet; see that it is I myself. Touch me and see, for a ghost does not have flesh and bones as you see that I have.'

And when he had said this, he showed them his hands and his feet. While in their joy they were disbelieving and still wondering, he said to them, 'Have you anything to eat?' They gave him a piece of grilled fish, and he took it and ate it in their presence.

Then he said to them, 'These are my words that I spoke to you while still with you – that everything written about me in the laws of Moses, the prophets and the psalms must be fulfilled.' Then he opened their minds to understand the scriptures, and he said to them, 'Thus it is written that the Messiah is to suffer and to rise from the dead on the third day, and that repentance and forgiveness of sins is to be proclaimed in his name to all nations, beginning from Jerusalem. You are witnesses of these things, and see I am sending you what my Father promised; so stay here in the city until you have been clothed with power from on high.'

Luke 24:35-48

COME, LORD JESUS

HERE WE HAVE the gospel reading for the 3rd Sunday of Easter, Year B, as well as Easter Thursday, a very rich scene indeed for our contemplation.

I slowly and attentively go through my usual preparation for contemplation. Our setting is an indoor one. The disciples, unlike Mary Magdalene or the two who took off for Emmaus, are shut away in fear and doubt, when they have three unexpected visitors. The two disciples who had left the community and gone off to Emmaus have come running back after recognising Jesus in the breaking of bread. What a story they have to tell, and how many questions their frightened and unbelieving confreres have to ask them! It is well worth pausing to contemplate the unbelieving disciples huddled together, and the two who have just returned, alive with enthusiasm.

And, suddenly, here is Jesus in our midst! There are no questions about how he got back from Emmaus or came through the locked doors. The risen Lord is in a new mode of existence, independent of space and time. As I begin to contemplate him in this mystery, I pray to know, love and follow him, as he walks with me on my mission to spread the joy of the Resurrection to all whom I meet. Though Jesus has now entered that new mode of existence, this scene will especially proclaim that his resurrection is truly a bodily reality.

Jesus begins with the usual Jewish greeting, a greeting so fitting for his risen life, 'Peace be with you.' On one level this is merely the common Middle Eastern greeting 'Shalom', but the gospel writers invest into it the mysterious life-giving power of the risen Lord. And how the disciples, and we, need the gift of this peace!

While we, of the third millennium, can take for granted realities like the Lord's suffering, death and resurrection, for them the frenetic pace of these realities, experienced for the first time, leads to doubt, fear and bewilderment. It is very appropriate that we too should experience similar emotions in so far as we need to open our hearts more to allowing the reality of the Lord's resurrection to totally transform all our living.

Jesus invites us, as he invited the disciples, to have the most intimate experience of touching his risen flesh. Like Thomas in the Lord's appearance to him, we may put our finger into the wounds of his hands and feet, and our hand into his opened side and heart. 'Their joy was so great that they could not believe it, and they stood there dumbfounded.'

This wonderful sentence underlines the reality that, like us, the disciples were not immediately raised to a state of unmitigated joy on seeing and even touching the Lord. So great was their joy that it continued to be mixed with unbelief. They could not find words to express the conflicting feelings going on inside them.

All human life requires a growth towards integration. It will take time for them to integrate into their lives the fact that the Lord whom they loved and followed so closely, whom they saw die so ignominiously, is now alive with a radically new kind of existence. Like St Paul, who wrote to the Philippians, 'All I want is to know Christ and the power of his resurrection', we are called to make the appropriation of the reality of the risen life of Jesus a truly lifelong quest.

We may well have already come to an authentic, living faith in the Lord's resurrection, but the living out of that faith in every aspect of our lives remains our challenge for the future. It became the reality of life for Paul, who wrote, 'For me, living is Christ' (Philippians 1:21) and 'It is no longer I who live, but it is Christ who lives in me' (Galatians 2:20).

Then comes perhaps the most startling part of our reading. Jesus asks for something to eat, and then eats a piece of grilled fish 'before their eyes'. Is Luke teaching his readers that the risen Lord, who is now in a new kind of existence, actually required and ate food. Perhaps he is! But it does seem more likely that this is simply Luke's way of emphasising that the Lord's resurrection is a truly bodily one.

There is so much symbolism in the resurrection stories that many Christians have come to assert that the resurrection is nothing more than a psychological revolution on the part of the disciples from disbelief to belief. Catholic faith proclaims that Jesus Christ is alive today in his fully human bodily existence, mysterious though that may be.

Luke now repeats for all the disciples the teaching of the road to Emmaus that the Lord brings to fulfilment the Law, the Prophets and the Psalms, and that this teaching is to spread out from Jerusalem to all the nations.

I pray to Mary, asking her to obtain from her Son a deepening of my faith in his bodily resurrection. I pray for a growing awareness of the depth of the mystery that Jesus is Lord of the Universe.

I come to Jesus and I profess my faith to him. I pray to the Father, Son and Holy Spirit, asking that my faith in the Resurrection of Jesus may sustain me in a truly joyful carrying out of my mission of being like my Lord in bringing good news to the poor.

— 31 —

The Risen Jesus and Mary of Magdala

In the gospel of John, the first person to meet Jesus on Easter Sunday morning was Mary Magdalene. Here is John's account of the meeting.

> But Mary stood weeping outside the tomb. As she wept, she bent over to look into the tomb; and she saw two angels in white sitting where the body of Jesus had been lying, one at the head and the other at the feet. They said to her, 'Woman, why are you weeping?' She said to them, 'They have taken away my Lord, and I do not know where they have laid him.'
>
> When she had said this, she turned around and saw Jesus standing there, but she did not know that it was Jesus. Jesus said to her, 'Woman, why are you weeping? Who are you looking for?' Supposing him to be the gardener, she said to him, 'Sir, if you have carried him away, tell me where you have laid him, and I will take him away.' Jesus said to her, 'Mary!' She turned and said to him in Hebrew, '*Rabbouni*' (which means Teacher).
>
> Jesus said to her, 'Do not hold on to me, because I have not yet ascended to the Father. But go to my brothers and say to them, I am ascending to my Father and your Father, to my God and your God.' Mary Magdalene went and told the disciples, 'I have seen the Lord'; and she told them that he had said these things to her.
>
> John 20:11-18

COME, LORD JESUS

THIS IS OUR GOSPEL for the Tuesday of Easter, and for the Memorial of Mary Magdalene (July 22). As we begin our Divine Reading and contemplation of this passage, we could begin by reflecting on the person of Mary Magdalene. She was in the news in recent years, thanks to the fiction of Dan Brown's *Da Vinci Code*.

Mary came from Magdala on the west bank of the Sea of Galilee. Traditionally she was identified with 'the woman who was a sinner' of the seventh chapter of Luke's gospel. But modern Scripture scholars point out that there is no reason for this identification except that Mary is mentioned immediately after that story at the start of the eighth chapter. There Luke writes about the women who were close disciples of Jesus: '... some women who had been cured of evil spirits and infirmities: Mary, called Magdalene, from whom seven demons had gone out, and Joanna, the wife of Herod's servant Chuza, and Susanna, and many others' (Luke 8:2). The 'seven demons' may refer to a cure from severe illness, and not to extreme sinfulness.

Mary became a totally committed disciple of Jesus. In fact, when it came to his suffering, death and resurrection, she has the most prominent part of all the disciples. She is the only person mentioned by Mark, Matthew and John as standing by the cross of Jesus. Again, she is the only person named by all four gospels as a participant in the events of the resurrection.

In our current text from John, Mary is the first person to bring the good news to Simon Peter, the 'beloved disciple' and the others. She is the first to whom Jesus appears, and Jesus personally commissions her to pass on his message to 'my brothers'.

We enter upon our contemplation by saying a brief prayer that all we do during this time may be to God's praise and glory. We become aware that Father, Son and Holy Spirit are here with us and in us now, as they were with Jesus and with Mary in

The Risen Jesus and Mary of Magdala

this scene. We allow our imagination to make us immediately present to the mystery we contemplate. We use our five senses. Perhaps taste and smell are a bit difficult! Ignatius of Loyola invites us to smell and taste the infinite fragrance and sweetness of the divinity! We see, hear and touch as Mary Magdalene and Jesus do.

Mary did not recognize Jesus at first. I don't recognize him immediately in the events of my daily life. But he is there if I let the realization dawn on me. It is only when Jesus pronounces her name – 'Mary!' – that she knows him. I hear him call me by name, lovingly, as my best friend. I may delay here for quite some time. I am reminded of the great words often repeated by Isaiah: 'I have called you by your name; you are mine' (Isaiah 43:1).

I picture Mary clinging to the knees of Jesus, just as Peter must have done when Jesus called him and he fell to his knees, saying, 'Depart from me, Lord, for I am a sinful man' (Luke 5:8). Mary Magdalene has found the risen Jesus, and never wants to let go of the experience. But the same Jesus who gives us intimate experiences of his presence also reminds us that we must 'let go'; we cannot cling to any experiences, but must get on with the often difficult work of spreading the Good News.

I, too, cling to him for as long as I like. I feel the touch of his embrace, as he hugs me as his best friend (even though, like Peter, I may be acutely aware of my unworthiness). Both aspects, the intimate encounter with Jesus and the mission he gives me, must be present if I want to be a true disciple of his.

At any point during the prayer I may be drawn to speak to Jesus or to Mary Magdalene, or just to be present with them.

Just as the Trinity was present with the risen Lord and with Mary Magdalene, the Father, the Son and the Holy Spirit are present to me now, and I may converse with each Person, just as I want to do as a result of this time spent in prayer.

— 32 —
My Lord and My God

One of the most important Gospel resurrection stories is the one we have as the gospel reading on the octave day of Easter: the apparition of Jesus to the apostle Thomas. It is read also on the feast of St Thomas (3 July).

> But Thomas (who was called the Twin), one of the twelve, was not with them when Jesus came. So the other disciples told him, 'We have seen the Lord.' But he said to them, 'Unless I see the mark of the nails in his hands, and put my finger into the mark of the nails and my hand into his side, I will not believe.'
> A week later his disciples were again in the house, and Thomas was with them. Although the doors were shut, Jesus came and stood among them and said, 'Peace be with you.' Then he said to Thomas, 'Put your finger here and see my hands. Reach out your hand and put it into my side. Do not doubt but believe.' Thomas answered him, 'My Lord and my God!' Jesus said to him, 'Have you believed because you have seen me? Blessed are those who have not seen me and yet have come to believe.'
>
> John 20:24-29

THE IMPORTANCE OF THIS passage is that, along with Luke's story about a meeting between Jesus and his disciples (Luke 24:38-43) it clearly affirms the bodily, physical character of the Lord's resurrection. What Luke wrote is:

> Jesus said to them, 'Why are you frightened, and why do doubts arise in your hearts? Look at my hands and my feet; see that it is I myself. Touch me and see; for a ghost does not have flesh and bones as you see that I have.' And when he had said this, he showed them his hands and his feet. While in their joy they were disbelieving and still wondering, he said to them, 'Have you anything here to eat?' They gave him a piece of grilled fish, and he took it and ate it before their eyes.

Was Luke teaching as historical fact that Jesus actually ate fish after his resurrection? There are several reasons for saying, 'most likely not'. But Luke was definitely teaching that Jesus rose bodily, and to emphasize this he used the symbol of eating.

Our passage from John is equally strong, or stronger, in its emphasis on the physicality of the resurrection. And it is free of the difficulties that the idea of the risen Lord's eating would arouse.

At the same time, the interchange between Jesus and Thomas gives us an exquisite scene of intimacy between the Lord and his apostle. We start our prayer with this gospel passage, as always, by composing ourselves through a brief time of relaxation and controlled breathing. The scene which has been well depicted in works of art is not difficult to imagine: Jesus standing with the wounds in his hands, feet and side clearly visible, Thomas kneeling in a posture of extreme awe and reverence, and reaching out to make the physical contact to which Jesus has invited him.

I may find it helpful to use a way of praying with the following focuses:

1. the persons;
2. what they say;
3. what they do;
4. reflect on myself and how this gospel passage relates to me.

1. So, first, I imagine Jesus in the reality of his risen Body, his wounds clearly visible. I see the look in his eyes, as he gazes at Thomas, as he gazes at me. This is the same risen Lord who is present with me now, and at every moment of my existence.

Then I focus on Thomas. He is a character very like Peter in the gospels, extrovert, self-confident, brash. 'Let us go up to Jerusalem with Jesus, so that we may die with him' (John 11, 16). 'Lord, we do not know where you are going. How can we know the way?' This prompted Jesus to say, 'I am the way' (John 14:5).

'Unless I see the mark of the nails in his hands, and put my finger into in the mark of the nails and my hand in his side, I will not believe' (John 20:25). Not very promising material, our Thomas. But what is the end result? The most exquisite profession of faith.

2. I hear what they say. Principally, the gentle, tender invitation of Jesus, responding to Thomas precisely in his weakness – his doubt. Moreover, Jesus reads the basic goodness and capacity for believing of Thomas, and so makes the extraordinary invitation to enter into his wounded hands and side.

So, there is evoked from Thomas the greatest profession of faith in all the gospels, 'My Lord and my God.' In all the writings of the four evangelists here is the only person to call Jesus God. It is ironic that Thomas is still generally referred to as 'doubting Thomas' when he is in fact the uniquely believing Thomas!

3. I see what they do. Does John imply that Thomas in fact did what Jesus invited him to do? I draw my own conclusions. Am I invited to a similar degree of unity with my risen Lord? Yes, I am. So, in my prayer I do whatever I am moved to do as I hear the same words of Jesus addressed to me. A golden opportunity for real intimacy with my Lord!

4. I reflect on myself. Here I have the words of Jesus about me personally: 'Blessed are they who have not seen and yet have come to believe.' I may be moved to profess my faith to Jesus.

Further I may be moved to put my finger into the mark of the nails in his hands, and my hand into his side. Clearly our contemplation is concerned with one of the greatest of all the Resurrection stories. Surely it provides us with ample scope to enter into conversation with Jesus, with Thomas, with the other disciples, with Mary and especially with Father, Son and Holy Spirit.

— 33 —
A Great Catch of Fish

After these things, Jesus showed himself again to his disciples by the Sea of Tiberias; and he showed himself in this way. Gathered there together were Simon Peter, Thomas called the Twin, Nathanael of Cana in Galilee, the sons of Zebedee, and two others of his disciples. Simon Peter said to them, 'I am going fishing.' They said to him, 'We will go with you.' They went out and got into the boat, but that night they caught nothing.

Just after daybreak, Jesus stood on the beach; but the disciples did not know that it was Jesus. Jesus said to them, 'Children, you have no fish, have you?' They answered him, 'No.' He said to them, 'Cast the net to the right side of the boat, and you will find some.' So they cast it, and now they were not able to haul it in because there were so many fish. That disciple whom Jesus loved said to Peter, 'It is the Lord!'

When Simon Peter heard that it was the Lord, he put on some clothes, for he was naked, and jumped into the sea. But the other disciples came in the boat, dragging the net full of fish, for they were not far from the land, only about a hundred yards off.

When they had gone ashore, they saw a charcoal fire there with fish on it, and bread. Jesus said to them, 'Bring some of the fish that you have just caught.' So Simon Peter went on board, and hauled the net ashore, full of large fish, a hundred and fifty-three of them, and though there were so many the net was not torn.

A Great Catch of Fish

> Jesus said to them, 'Come and have breakfast.' Now, none of the disciples dared to ask him 'Who are you?' because they knew that it was the Lord. Jesus came and took some bread and gave it to them, and did the same with the fish. This was now the third time that Jesus appeared to the disciples after he was raised from the dead.
>
> John 21:1-14

THIS IS THE GOSPEL for the 3rd Sunday of Easter, Year C, and Friday of the 1st Week of Easter.

Chapter 21 of John is an appendix to a gospel which had been formally closed by the last words of chapter 20. The scribe may be a different one in the Joannine school, or perhaps the same one who wrote the rest of the gospel. As in Mark and Matthew, but not Luke, the setting for the apparition to the disciples is their home province of Galilee. Not only are they to meet the risen Lord in returning home, but in returning to the ordinariness of their occupation as fishermen.

The scene for our contemplation is readily imaginable. We can see the Sea of Tiberias (or Lake of Galilee), where so much of the Lord's pre-resurrection life was lived. We begin praying, as always, to know, love and follow Jesus better.

As we usually do in our gospel contemplations, we may be greatly helped by seeing in imagination the persons of the Trinity as they gaze upon Jesus, and those disciples whom they love carrying out their mission for the salvation of all humankind. As they do, we look with love upon Jesus, and all that he says and does in this mystery.

We see the persons in the scene: first of all Jesus, different now, but the same person we have got to know, love and follow in all his earthly mysteries. Now he appears as a mysterious figure on the shore. His identity is not hidden from us, and we ask him, as in all his earthly mysteries, for that growth in relationship which means knowing, loving and following him more devotedly. Perhaps, like the disciples, we too notice something different about the risen Jesus.

During his earthly life he was a man busy on mission, always involved in teaching and healing, always on the move to reach out to more and more people. Now he is no longer so busy. His role seems to have changed from that of hard-working teacher and healer to one of being a listener-responder. Now more even than before he is conscious of the inner life of each person, and with exquisite courtesy responds to each one just as they need him. Here he simply becomes involved in the chore of preparing a barbeque for his famished friends, who laboured all night and caught nothing.

We see the disciples who are named, most of them familiar to us, especially Peter and the beloved disciple. They are at a loose end, reminiscent of Luke's pair going off to Emmaus. They jump at the chance to be busy and take up Peter's suggestion of returning to the old life of fishing.

We gradually linger over watching what each person is doing – Jesus preparing the barbeque, each of the disciples taking his appropriate part in the fishing expedition, their hard work for no result. We notice them let out their nets once more in answer to the stranger's advice. Then the great catch. A hundred and fifty-three big fish! For all their work scripture scholars are none the wiser about any significance in the number! We see Peter return to the boat at the invitation of Jesus, haul the net ashore, and bring some of the fish for the breakfast.

Then we see Jesus come and take the bread and give it to them, and then do the same with the fish. We are reminded of the very same words in a Eucharistic context in John 6:11, 'Then Jesus took the loaves, and when he had given thanks he distributed them to those who were seated; so also the fish, as much as they wanted.' The loaves come first; the fish are of secondary importance.

We listen to what each of the persons in this mystery of the risen Lord had to say. Only eight very short sentences, and each one about the simple reality of the fishing expedition and the barbequed breakfast, except for one. The beloved disciple says to Peter, 'It is the Lord.' Recognition of the risen Lord seems always to be difficult.

As, in the words of St Ignatius, I reflect upon myself to draw fruit, I may notice the same difficulty. As with Peter and the beloved disciple, we need to help one another to recognize the presence of the risen Lord in events, situations and feelings where he is not immediately obvious. The making of a review of our day in an awareness examen each evening can be a great help in this process of becoming more aware of the Lord's constant presence.

As we are drawn to it, we enter into conversation with Mary and with Jesus, We ask them to present us to the Father. Perhaps we can converse also with the Father, or dwell over what we say so often in the Lord's Prayer, prayed in union with Jesus, in the Holy Spirit.

— 34 —

I Am the Way

Jesus said to his disciples, 'Do not let your hearts be troubled. Believe in God, believe also in me. In my Father's house there are many dwelling places. If it were not so, would I have told you that I go to prepare a place for you? And if I go and prepare a place for you, I will come again and take you to myself, so that where I am there you may be also. And you know the way to the place where I am going.'

Thomas said to him, 'Lord, we do not know where you are going. How can we know the way?' Jesus said to him, 'I am the way, and the truth, and the life. No one comes to the Father except through me. If you know me, you will know my Father also. From now on you do know him and have seen him.'

Philip said to him, 'Lord, show us the Father, and we will be satisfied.' Jesus said to him, 'Have I been with you all this time, Philip, and you still do not know me? Whoever has seen me has seen the Father. How can you say, "Show us the Father"? Do you not believe that I am in the Father, and the Father is in me? The words I say to you I do not speak on my own; but the Father who dwells in me does his works. Believe me that I am in the Father, and the Father is in me; but, if you do not, believe me because of the works themselves.

'Very truly, I tell you, the one who believes in me will also do the works that I do and, in fact, will do greater works than these, because I am going to the Father. I

I Am the Way

will do whatever you ask in my name, so that the Father may be glorified in the Son. If in my name you ask me anything, I will do it.'

John 14:1-14

THIS IS THE GOSPEL of the 5th Sunday of Easter, Year A.

In the gospel of John the discourse of Jesus at the Last Supper, along with his great prayer of chapter 17, offer us material which invites us to be contemplative. Concrete presence to persons and actions is somewhat limited, but the words themselves are deep and specially rich in meaning. We go through our usual approach to contemplative prayer. We make our preparatory offering of our prayer time; we enter in imagination into the setting, and we ask the Lord that we may know, love and follow him more devotedly.

Perhaps we are more aware than usual of the presence of Father, Son and Holy Spirit as they look upon Jesus in the final stages of his preparation to leave his disciples and this Earth. They look specially upon me too as I listen to Jesus speak about the life of the Trinity that I share through baptism. I am, of course, intensely present to Jesus as he utters these great words, as well as to the Father and the Holy Spirit, who are the focus of what Jesus is saying. I may wish to be present also to friends of mine among the apostles, or to those two heroes of John's, Thomas and Philip, who share in this scene, along with Jude.

Jesus, aware of how upset the disciples are when he speaks of leaving them, starts his discourse with words of encouragement about their future, the same words that have encouraged so many at Christian funerals: 'Do not let your hearts be troubled. In my Father's house there are many dwelling places, and I am going to prepare a place for you.' When Jesus declares that they know the way to the place where he is going, the brash Thomas says, 'We don't even know where you are going, so how can we know the way?' The reply of Jesus is a favourite saying of very many – 'I am the way, the truth, and the life.' However, it is often misunderstood, as if the three are equivalent. Jesus is in effect saying I am the Way.

In the Acts, the expression 'the Way' is often repeated by Luke as a name for the church, the Christian way of life. In Mark, Bartimaeus, after his healing, followed Jesus in the Way. Jesus is the way because he is full of truth and of life. For John, life, love, peace, joy, truth, freedom are all gifts of the Spirit which Jesus shares to the full.

John now gives a contemplative explanation of what Jesus will say in chapter 17: 'This is eternal life, to know you, the only true God, and Jesus Christ whom you have sent.' To know Jesus is to know the Father, and, in answer to Philip's intervention, to have seen Jesus is to have seen the Father. This is not only true for the disciples, but for each of us who contemplates.

To see Jesus with the eyes of our imagination is not 'just imagination'. It is to be in intimate personal contact with him, and with the Father, and with the Holy Spirit. The persons of the Trinity are not remote from us, but are really accessible through the use of our spiritual senses. This has been the teaching of Fathers of the Church for centuries, but sadly not well understood, because not often sufficiently explained. Not only Philip, but each of us is invited by Jesus to affirm that we have seen the Father.

The author of the first letter of John was not the 'disciple who had reclined on the breast of Jesus at the Last Supper', but a later scribe of the same school. He affirms in his prologue that he saw Jesus (no fewer than four times in his first three verses). He saw him, not 'in the flesh' but in his contemplation. He also heard and touched the Lord!

I Am the Way

Jesus declares that he speaks the words he is speaking because the Father is living in him, and accomplishing his works. For John, Jesus is essentially the one sent by the Father. Whatever words he speaks, whatever works he accomplishes, it is all because the Father is working in and through him. Work is another great theme of John's gospel. Jesus is always at work, until the last moment, when he declares on the cross, 'It is finished.' He had completed the work the Father sent him to accomplish.

Not only are Jesus and the Father at work, but we, those believing into him, will do greater works than Jesus has done. We will do this because Jesus is 'going to the Father'. When he does go to the Father, the Holy Spirit will bring to its fulfilment the life of the Trinity in us, God's people, and the work of bringing about the coming of God's kingdom will really flourish. Not only our work but our prayer will be effective instruments in the coming of the kingdom.

The kind of prayer that will accomplish this is, in the words of Jesus, 'prayer in my name', that is, prayer in which we attend to our personal relationship with Jesus living within us, and allow that indwelling to accomplish its purpose. 'If in my name you ask me for anything, I will do it.'

As we conclude this contemplation, it may be an excellent time to practise 'prayer in the name of Jesus'. Can I have some experience of his living in me, of my union with him. If so, let me ask him not so much for what I want, but for what he wants to grace me with, as I contemplate his indwelling. Or, in the words of the Lord's Prayer, which I pray 'in the name of Jesus', let me pray for the coming of his kingdom.

— 35 —
You Are My Friends

'I am the vine, and my Father is the vine grower. He removes every branch in me that bears no fruit. Every branch that bears fruit he prunes to make it bear more fruit. You have already been cleansed by the word I have spoken to you. Abide in me as I abide in you. Just as the branch cannot bear fruit by itself unless it abides in the vine, neither can you unless you abide in me. I am the vine, you are the branches. Those who abide in me and I in them bear much fruit, because without me you can do nothing.

'Whoever does not abide is me is thrown away like a branch and withers; such branches are gathered, thrown into the fire and burned. If you abide in me and my words abide in you, ask for whatever you wish and it will be done for you. My Father is glorified by this, that you bear much fruit and become my disciples. As the Father has loved me, so I have loved you; abide in my love. If you keep my commandments, you will abide in my love, just as I have kept my Father's commandments and abide in his love. I have said these things to you so that my joy may be in you, and your joy may be complete.

'This is my commandment, that you love one another as I have loved you. No one has greater love than this, to lay down one's life for one's friends. You are my friends if you do what I command you. I do not call you servants any longer, because the servant does not know what the master is doing; but I have called you friends, because I have made known to you everything that I have learned from my Father. You did not choose me but I chose you. And I appointed you to go and bear fruit, fruit that will last, so that the Father will give you whatever you ask him in my name, I am giving you these commands so that you will love one another.'

John 15:1-17

VERSES 1-8 ARE THE GOSPEL for the 5th Sunday of Easter, Year B, and verses 9-17 are the gospel for the 6th Sunday of Easter, Year B.

As with our previous contemplations, we begin by settling ourselves for the time of prayer by attention to our deep breathing or some other awareness exercise. We stand in God's presence just near the place in which we are about to pray; we look steadily at it as a special place where we are going to meet the Lord and grow in union with him for the carrying out of our mission. We make our preparatory prayer by offering to him this time of prayer, all we are and all that we will do, solely for his glory and the coming of his kingdom.

We begin to reflect on the grace of our Baptism, our union with Father, Son and Holy Spirit, in whose presence we are. If it should happen that we are captured by this presence of God, or of one of the Persons of the Trinity, we stay there without moving on: this could well be the grace the Lord prepared for us in this prayer, and we don't want to rush past it.

If we are not so captured, let us, like Ignatius, the great man of prayer, turn to Mary our Mother who is vitally interested in our well being and our relationship with her Son, as well as with the Spirit, and the Father. We ask for her help, which she is only too ready to give, and perhaps ask her to bring us to Jesus, so that our relationship with him may become more alive for us at this time.

As we pray to Jesus, it often happens that we become more ready to attend to Father, eternal Son, or Holy Spirit, and to pour out to any or all of them what is most on our mind and in our heart right now.

We may choose to enter on the subject matter of our prayer by way of *Lectio Divina* or by following Ignatius's simple instructions of being present via our imagination, and seeing the persons, hearing what they are saying, and contemplating what they are doing, then reflecting on our own lives to see how the grace contained in this particular Word of God is to influence us.

Jesus begins this part of the discourse about his union with his disciples and with us, by speaking to them about his relationship with his Father. 'I am the vine, and my Father is the vine grower.' Throughout the gospel of John, he is always conscious of being the one sent by the Father. Here the emphasis is more on the way the Father has shared his life with him, right from the moment of his conception to this moment of imminent death.

What gratitude there is in the heart of Jesus! He is not alone in being nurtured by the Father. So are we; and the Father displays to each of us 'tough love' through the painful process of pruning involved in the sufferings of our lives, so that we may bear more fruit. How important to have this right perspective on the suffering inevitable for every human being, and for me in particular. No matter what the course of events for us, we are to abide in Jesus, that is, to live in him, to be constantly aware that he and I are one.

This leads Jesus back to the beginning of this chapter, but now with special reference to us: 'I am the vine, and you are the branches.' We are reminded that we must keep growing in this divine union; if we don't, we will wither. Our life of union with the Lord must constantly grow or we will die. And Jesus is on the side of constant growth; 'my Father is glorified in this, that you bear much fruit and become my disciples.'

Jesus loves every one of us. He masterfully sets up the paradigm for human loving in verses 9 and 12: 'As the Father has loved me, so I have loved you' and 'Love one another as I have loved you.' Do you mean, Lord, that my love for Bill or Anne or Rosie or George is to be the same as the Father's infinite love for you? 'Yes, that is what I said. And it is totally possible when you abide in me as I abide in you' (verse 4).

No other evangelist writes about joy to the extent that John does. Joy, for John, is like the icing on the cake. He writes about it towards the end of the gospel, and towards the end of particular sections. How could we possibly doubt that, as we contemplate the profound truths of love and union, so intimately expounded by Jesus, we must experience overflowing joy? 'No one has greater love than this, to lay down one's life for one's friends.' It happens often in our world. There are even those who die in trying to save complete strangers.

'You are my friends.' Jesus goes on to spell out the significance of this relationship in declaring that there are no secrets hidden from us. He has shared with us everything he has learned from his Father; there are no secrets in our relationship.

To be a friend of Jesus is to be both called and sent. That friendship is not a smothering, exclusive one; it involves always being on mission for the coming of the kingdom, in the words of Jesus, 'to bear much fruit, fruit that will endure'. Then we have the same climax as in chapter 14. Prayer in the name of Jesus, that is, prayer that arises out of our attentiveness to our abiding in union with him, will infallibly be answered (verse 16). The same will be spelled out again in John 16:23-24.

COME, LORD JESUS

With these words of Jesus concerning the infallibility of prayer still in our ears, I turn to Mary; I converse with her: I listen and I speak; I ask her to lead me into the company of her Son. I pray to him to help me have a deep, contemplative appreciation of abiding in him like a branch in a vine.

May I go further, and ask him to gift me with an experience of that union; and then to lead me into the presence of the Father to pour out my gratitude in the Holy Spirit for all that a life of contemplative prayer means to me.

— 36 —

Life in Abundance

'Very truly, I tell you, anyone who does not enter the sheepfold by the gate but climbs in another way is a thief and a bandit. The one who enters by the gate is the shepherd of the sheep. The gatekeeper opens the gate for him, and the sheep hear his voice. He calls his own sheep by name, and he leads them out. When he has called his own out, he goes ahead of them, and the sheep follow him because they know his voice. They will not follow a stranger, but they will run from him, because they do not know the voice of strangers.'

Jesus used this figure of speech with them, but they did not understand what he was saying to them.

So again Jesus said to them, 'Very truly, I tell you. I am the gate for the sheep. All who came before me are thieves and bandits; but the sheep did not listen to them. I am the gate. Whoever enters by me will be saved, and will come in and go out and find pasture. The thief comes only to steal and kill and destroy. I came that they may have life, and have it abundantly.'

John 10:1-10

THIS IS THE GOSPEL for the 4th Sunday of Easter, Year A, and Monday of the 4th Week of Easter.

We are all familiar with the metaphor of God as shepherd of God's people in the Old Testament; also of Jesus as shepherd in the New Testament; and of ministers of the gospel as pastors, or shepherds, in modern times. Some may not be flattered when asked to consider themselves as sheep, but the persistence of the metaphor through the ages surely means that it provides us with sure grounds for fruitful contemplation.

It is a truism to say that the contemplative life is fostered by presence to nature. To be in touch with the beauty of creation at sunrise or sunset, or in the soft glow of moonlight, or in gazing at the stars (a favourite habit of St Ignatius during his 'shut in' days in Rome), or in resting upon rocks and viewing the rolling waves by the seashore. All of these provide our contemplative spirit with ample material to raise our minds and hearts.

What is true of nature on the grand scale is also true of a contemplative presence to something really tiny, to something new or something old. The great Jesuit palaeontologist, Pierre Teilhard de Chardin, had a passionate love of the ancient rocks that fed his very contemplative heart and mind.

Whatever is true of inanimate nature is *a fortiori* true of our relationship with living creatures. The ancient trees, the colourful flowers, the variegated beauty of the rain forest can all speak to us of the beauty of the Creator.

When we move our attention to the animal kingdom, the scope for contemplation broadens into new dimensions. The strength of the tiger or lion, the elephant or whale, the speed and grace of the cheetah, the rare beauty of the kangaroo or koala, and so on the cavalcade continues, until we come to our special subject, the lowly sheep.

Sheep symbolize for us poverty of spirit. They are weak, gentle and meek; they lack power and speed and even grace. Their diet is the utterly bland one of endless grass. They are totally dependent on the shepherd to protect them from the ravenous wolf and other predators, to keep them together in a flock, for warmth and protection and security. They are vulnerable in so many ways, and even seem quite incompetent at dealing with their vulnerability.

These are the creatures whom God chose to be symbols of God's people. But, further, God chose them to be symbols of the glorified Christ, the Lamb to whom the great hymn of the book of Revelation is sung: 'You are worthy to take the scroll and open its seals, for you were slaughtered and by your blood you ransomed for God saints from every tribe and language and people and nation; you have made them to be a kingdom and priests, serving our God, and they will reign on earth' (Revelation 5:9-10). And, later, 'To the one seated on the throne and to the Lamb be blessing and honour and glory and might forever and ever' (Revelation 5:13).

In the Old Testament, we have everybody's favourite, Psalm 23. In it, David, the former shepherd, gives expression to a profound, contemplative intimacy between the Lord and himself, an intimacy all of us share in as we recite and ponder this great psalm. Ezekiel, after denouncing the false shepherds of God's people, Israel, gives us a wonderful, lyrical account of how the Lord God will attend to the shepherding of God's own sheep. Once again the most striking element is the intimacy displayed by God in God's respect for the sheep (Ezekiel 34:11-16).

In the New Testament, the key reading is our present one, along with its continuation through verses 11 to 18. In these readings are three of the great 'I am' (the word of God to Moses at the burning bush) sayings. Jesus proclaims, 'I am the gate of the sheepfold' (verse 7); 'I am the gate' (verse 8); and 'I am the good shepherd. I know my own and my own know me, just as the Father knows me and I know the Father' (verses 14-15).

The intimacy of the Old Testament is continued and deepened. We humans often express intimacy in saying, 'It's wonderful to see your face', or, 'It's wonderful to hear your voice.' The sheep are the same. They are happy to hear the voice of Jesus, their shepherd, and they reject other voices.

We have the brief but compelling love of the shepherd in the parable of the lost sheep (Luke 15:4-7). In his utterly extravagant love this shepherd will leave ninety-nine untended in order to go after the one which has strayed. Isn't this foolish? Couldn't the ninety-nine come to harm? This is the language of reason, but the language of the good shepherd is a different one: the language of love.

Finally we have the role of the pastors of the church, as they share in St Peter's commission after the resurrection. 'Feed my lambs; look after my sheep. Feed my sheep', said Jesus, in continuing his own mission. 'I have come that they may have life, and have it abundantly [or, to the full]' (John 10:10).

In acknowledging myself to be a sheep of Jesus, the good shepherd, I desire to embrace poverty of spirit. This is only possible as an outcome of a received grace. I come to Mary to ask her to bring me to Jesus to receive this grace.

Then, with Ignatius, I pray in their presence for them to bring me to Father, Son and Holy Spirit, so that I may be assured of the reception of this poverty of spirit, which is, in fact, life in abundance.

— 37 —
Father, Glorify Your Name

After Jesus had spoken these words, he looked up to heaven and said, 'Father, the hour has come; glorify your Son so that the Son may glorify you, since you have given him authority over all people, to give eternal life to all you have given him. And this is eternal life, that they may know you, the only true God, and Jesus Christ whom you have sent. I glorified you on earth by finishing the work you gave me to do.

'So now, Father, glorify me in your own presence with the glory that I had in your presence before the world existed. I have made your name known to those whom you gave me from the world. They were yours, and you gave them to me, and they have kept your word. Now they know that everything you have given me is from you; for the words that you gave me I have given to them, and they have received them and know in truth that I came from you; and they have believed that you sent me.

'I am asking on their behalf; I am not asking on behalf of the world, but on behalf of those whom you gave me, because they are yours. All mine are yours, and yours are mine; and I have been glorified in them.

'And, now, I am no longer in the world, but they are in the world, and I coming to you. Holy Father, protect them in your name that you have given to me, so that they may be one as we are one.

John 17:1-11

IN THE LITURGY, this is the reading for the 7th Sunday of Easter, Year A, and also for the Tuesday of the 7th Week of Easter.

It is hard to imagine anything more suitable for contemplation than this 'priestly prayer' of Jesus. In it the great contemplative writer of John's gospel gives us the last prayer of Jesus as a legacy to his disciples. The prayer contains John's profound teaching on Trinitarian life as it is shared with them and us. We are put into immediate touch with the Jesus who is praying, with the Holy Spirit through whom the prayer is accomplished and with the Father to whom it is addressed.

As we enter upon our contemplation in the presence of Father, Son and Holy Spirit, hopefully we will have a ready access to the Divine Persons as we focus our imagination upon Jesus praying in the Holy Spirit to the Father.

Let us commence with a few general and contextual observations. This prayer of Jesus may well be called the Lord's Prayer in John. All the great prayers of Jesus in the New Testament are really the one prayer. In Luke and Matthew we have the two versions of the Lord's Prayer, as we know it. In that prayer, there are three essential parts: the address to the Father; prayer concerning the Father's glory; and prayer for our needs. These three parts are present in the Gethsemane prayer of Mark, Matthew and Luke, as in this prayer of John. In fact, the address 'Father' occurs in this chapter of John no less than six times. This relationship with God as Father is the essence of all true Christian prayer.

In his opening address to the Father, Jesus sets the context for his great prayer – 'Father, the hour has come.' These are very poignant words, as they refer to the imminent death of Jesus, but they refer also to his coming glory. For John, the word 'hour' refers to the hour for him to pass out of this world to the Father (John 13:1). This is the completion of the movement in the great theological prologue of John's gospel, where the Word, who was God, with the Father from eternity, came into this world in being 'made flesh'.

So now Jesus prays to the Father 'glorify your Son', not for his own sake, but for ours, in order that the Son may glorify the Father by giving eternal life to 'all you have given him'.

Of the three petitions concerning the Father in our Lord's Prayer, this prayer of John 17 is dominated by the prayer, 'hallowed be your name' in the form 'glorify your name'. 'Hallowed be your name', along with 'your kingdom come' and 'your will be done', point to one and the same reality, namely 'share your life with your people', or 'give us eternal life' ('on earth as it is in heaven').

John's gospel belongs to the end of the first century, the era of the rampant Gnostic heresy. Gnosticism is a theory that salvation belongs to those who have a special kind of esoteric knowledge, not shared by ordinary people. John refutes this heresy by appealing to a new and authentic knowledge available to all. 'This is eternal life that they may know you, the only true God, and Jesus Christ whom you have sent.'

In our contemplation this is a wonderful point in which to rest, praying really to know Jesus, and through him the Father. In doing this we are activating the prayer of Ignatius in his contemplation of the Gospel, namely to know, love and follow our Lord in each of his mysteries.

Jesus now professes that he has finished the work the Father gave him to do on earth, so glorifying God. He will repeat this in his last words on the cross: 'It is consummated [completed].' Now he prays for his own personal glorification in the presence of the Father forever, not for the glorification of divinity, but for the glorification the Father had in store for him in his humanity since eternity.

'I have made your name known' (verse 6).' In the gospel

of John there are no fewer than thirteen examples of Jesus' declaring 'I am', the same name that God had declared to Moses at the burning bush. The most striking among these are: 'Before Abraham was, I am.' 'When I am lifted up from the earth you will know that I am.' When walking on the water, 'Fear not; I am'.

This is one way in which Jesus has made the Father's name known to the disciples. But there is more to it than that. By revealing to them who he is, Jesus reveals the Father to them. He has done this by sharing his life and therefore the Father's life with his disciples. He now promises to go on sharing that life, and so making known the Father's 'name' in his coming glorification.

Jesus now turns to what preoccupies him at this time of approaching death, the preservation of his disciples. The rest of John 17 will be dominated by prayer for them, and then prayer for us who are the beneficiaries of their divine mission. They are his because they have been entrusted to him by the Father, to whom they really belong.

The whole of this chapter has a double perspective. It is written post-resurrection, and in this regard is very positive about the apostles: 'They have kept your word' (verse 6); 'Now they know' (verse 7); 'They know in truth that I came from you' (verse 8); 'I have been glorified in them' (verse 10). A short time ago (John 16:30), the disciples were claiming, 'Now we know', and Jesus in effect rebuked them, and told them they didn't know. In its real time frame his prayer is pre-Passion, so Jesus must pray for their preservation and salvation. They are 'in the world' so they, and we, are very much in need of this prayer of Jesus, in order that we be 'kept safe in the time of trial' , as we pray in the last petition of the Lord's Prayer.

Jesus now concludes this first section of his prayer, recalling his basic plea to the Father, the equivalent of 'hallowed be thy name' and applying it to his prayer for the disciples: 'Holy Father, protect them in your name, so that they may be one as we are one.'

I turn to Father, Son and Holy Spirit to converse with each of them, or simply to remain in their presence as I make the prayer of Jesus my own. As Jesus has just asked the Father for a unity among his disciples like their union, I may want to ask that I have the same union with those whom I love, and who love me.

— 38 —
Safe from the Evil One

'And now I am no longer in the world, but they are in the world, and I am coming to you. Holy Father, protect them in your name that you have given me, so that they may be one, as we are one.

'While I was with them, I protected them in your name that you have given me. I guarded them, and not one is lost; except the one destined to be lost, so that the scripture might be fulfilled. But now I am coming to you, and I speak these things in the world so that they may have my joy made complete in themselves.

'I have given them your word, and the world has hated them because they do not belong to the world, just as I do not belong to the world. I am not asking you to take them out of the world, but I ask you to protect them from the evil one. They do not belong to the world, just as I do not belong to the world.

'Sanctify them in the truth; your word is truth. As you have sent me into the world, so I have sent them into the world. And for their sake I sanctify myself, so that they also may be sanctified in truth.'

John 17:11-19

THIS CONTINUATION OF the prayer of Jesus in John 17 is the gospel for Wednesday of the 7th Week of Easter.

Once again we become aware of our presence to Jesus as he prays in the company of his disciples. We offer our preparatory prayer, and compose ourselves for contemplation by being present in imagination to Jesus and his disciples as he prays with them before going out to approach his coming arrest.

The first part of the prayer of John (John 17:1-11) is celebrated in the liturgy the day before. In that first part, the basic theme of the prayer is addressed, and already Jesus begins to pray for his disciples. Now he goes on to deepen that prayer on their behalf.

We pray to know, love and follow Jesus all the way to Calvary in union with him, as he is in union with Father, Son and Holy Spirit. One cannot stress too much the unity of this prayer with the synoptics' Lord's Prayer (Luke chapter 11 and Matthew chapter 6) and with the synoptics' prayer of Jesus before his Passion. It seems that John 17 is located at the table of the Last Supper, but at the end of chapter 14 John did quote Jesus as saying, 'Rise, let us be on our way.'

Our chapter (17) takes place immediately before Jesus goes out to cross the Kedron valley to his arrest in 18:1. This place is called by John a garden. It is from this verse that the first sorrowful mystery of the rosary was named 'the agony in the garden'. The prayer of Jesus in John 17 is more fully spelt out, but is the same prayer in essence as the prayer of Jesus in Gethsemane in Mark and Matthew and on the Mount of Olives in Luke. Like John 17, these last three occur immediately before the arrest.

This section of the prayer begins with the statement of Jesus that he is in the process of leaving the world, but his disciples are still in the world. The word 'world' has two distinct and opposite meanings in John's gospel: a very positive one, as in the famous text of John 3:16: 'God so loved the world that God gave God's only begotten Son so that everyone who believes into him may not perish, but may have eternal life.'

The second, negative, meaning points to those people who were the enemies threatening the existence of John's community. The first letter of John sees the spirit of the world as the spirit of Antichrist, the root of evil: 'All that is in the world is the desire of the flesh, the desire of the eyes, and pride in riches (2:16). Jesus needs to pray for his disciples' protection from the spirit of the world, which seeks to divide them from one another.

Jesus prays, therefore, not only that they remain together as a human community, but that their union is as deep and powerful as the union of Father and Son: 'Protect them in your name, so that they may be one as we are one' (verse 11). Later in the prayer, in the section in which Jesus will pray for all future believers (from verse 20 on), the theme of union will be thoroughly treated. But at this stage the emphasis is still on protection for the disciples and their warding off of the influences which tend to destroy their union. 'While I was with them I protected them in your name' – that is, I fostered their personal relationship with you.

One of the basic themes of John's gospel is the revelation by Jesus of who he is, in order to reveal who the Father is. This revelation is not a revealing of abstract theological truths; it is a revelation of the Father as one who is in close personal relationship with them, the one whose life they share. The mission is rightly seen as a concrete one of sharing the Father's love with them, and so revealing who he is, which will lead the author of the first letter of John to be able to write 'God is love' (1 John 4:16). Jesus refers to the loss of Judas, just one out of the twelve under his special care – a very good retention rate!

Jesus announces that his purpose in speaking out this prayer is that the disciples may experience the fullness of his joy in themselves. John writes often about joy, usually towards the end of a section of the gospel, or towards the end of the gospel itself.

He goes on to say, 'I have given them your word.' Occasionally there are references to 'words' in the plural, but, more often to the singular 'word', something giving concrete expression to the inner depth of a person. Words are all very well, but in verse 20 he will pray for those who will believe through their word, that is, through their living witness.

'I am not asking you to take them out of the world, but I ask you to protect them from the evil one.' The same Greek expression can be translated 'evil' (in general) or 'the evil one'. The same applies to the last line of Matthew's Lord's Prayer.

In keeping with the great personal emphasis of Scripture, both the good and the bad, 'the evil one' is preferred. For Luke the last words of the Lord's Prayer are, 'do not bring us to the time of trial.' This is a vital prayer for protection against those great, cosmic forces of evil that threaten to destroy our faith. It was what the disciples in Gethsemane were told to pray for by Jesus.

In his Lord's Prayer, Matthew adds: 'but deliver us from the evil one.' Both these prayers are about the one reality. Here John completes the parallel with the Lord's Prayer by the introduction of the prayer to keep them safe from the evil one: 'Father, glorify your name, keep them safe from the evil one.'

The final words of this section – 'for their sake I sanctify myself, so that they too may be sanctified in truth' – are a priestly formula, from which John 17 is often referred to as the 'high priestly prayer of Jesus'. Let us conclude by turning in prayer to Mary, to Jesus himself, and in so far as we are drawn, to each of the three Divine Persons.

The great prayer of Jesus we have just contemplated has the constant focus of union with Father, Son and Holy Spirit; so it should not be difficult for us to focus on these three personal relationships, which are always at the heart of all our prayer as baptized Christians striving to live out that baptism in all the complex and challenging relationships of our lives on this planet.

— 39 —
The Ascension

> Now the eleven disciples went to Galilee, to the mountain to which Jesus had directed them. When they saw him, they worshipped him; but some doubted. And Jesus came and said to them, 'All authority in heaven and on earth has been given to me. Go therefore and make disciples of all the nations, baptizing them into the name of the Father and of the Son, and of the Holy Spirit, and teaching them to obey everything that I have commanded you. And, remember, I am with you always, to the end of the age.'
>
> Matthew 28:16-20

THIS IS OUR GOSPEL READING for Trinity Sunday (Year B) as well as for the Solemnity of the Ascension, Year A.

It is remarkable that this should be chosen when there is no account of an ascension, but rather an account of the 'abiding with' of Jesus. Moreover, it takes place, not in the traditional place where Luke locates the Lord's ascension, Mt Olivet near Jerusalem, but rather in distant Galilee. What did actually happen, and where? These are bogus questions. The evangelists are not primarily interested in geography, nor in history as we understand that term, but rather in profound mystery. Happily, this is what provides material for our contemplation.

We go through the usual preparatory steps to be ready to contemplate. As we call to mind the setting, we are present on

The Ascension

Matthew's unnamed mountain in Galilee. We are reminded of two other Matthean mountains in Galilee, the mount of the Beatitudes and the mount of the Transfiguration. Why in Galilee? It is in a return to their home, their place of ordinary living that they will encounter the risen Lord, rather than in the exotic experiences of the heady days in Jerusalem.

In Matthew's gospel, the angel said to the women at the tomb on Easter day, 'tell his disciples he has been raised from the dead, and indeed he is going ahead of you to Galilee; there you will see him.' (Matthew 28:7). For John (chapter 21) the encounter will take place not only in a return to Galilee, but in going back to their former occupation of fishing. Perhaps we too are called to meet him at home in the ordinary rather than in some special circumstances or experiences.

We see the eleven disciples, the familiar twelve apostles minus Judas. We too may wish to focus on Jesus and to fall down in adoration before him. 'But some doubted.'

The phrase is not intended to lead us into the irrelevancy of wondering which ones. Rather it highlights the fact that the Resurrection appearances are not all 'sweetness and light'. Repeatedly they include elements of fear, doubt, grief, disbelief, etc., even in the midst of the predominant peace and joy. So too with us: we are called to find the presence of the Lord Jesus in the whole gamut of the human emotions we experience.

In the very act of the disciples' doubting, Jesus drew nearer and spoke to them. He is indeed universal Lord: 'All authority in heaven and on earth has been given to me.' He then shares with them, believers and doubters alike, his universal mission: 'Go and make disciples of all the nations.' Little did the disciples realize then what was involved. For them 'all the nations' would mean only the tiny area around the Mediterranean familiar to them. Perhaps their reaction was simplistically gung-ho. They must learn through their experience of all the ups and downs of their apostolic lives what it means to be an authentic Christian on mission.

The mission given to the eleven disciples was to make disciples and to baptize into the name of the Father and of the Son and of the Holy Spirit. No doubt Matthew is here quoting the liturgical formula already in use in the church at the time of his writing. But what does it mean?

In English, the phrase 'in the name of' normally means 'on behalf of' or 'with the authority of'. That is not what is meant here. The meaning is conveyed by the preposition 'into' (Greek *eis*). Had Matthew meant to convey the normal meaning of the English phrase 'in the name of', he would have used the word 'in' (Greek *en*). Why do English translators not write 'into the name of'? Because this is not a normal English expression. But the reality which it is expressing is not normal. It is that unique relationship of personal union at our deepest level with the Trinity.

We are baptized into intimate personal relationship with Father, Son and Holy Spirit. For the Jews (and Matthew is the most Jewish of the four gospels) 'the name' is sacred and demands the deepest respect; it means the reality of the person in all of that person's power.

To be a disciple of Jesus is to be in profound personal relationship with him in the power of the Spirit. The baptismal formula gives expression to that reality of spiritual union with Father, Son and Holy Spirit, a mystery only accessible to us through profound, ongoing contemplation. The mission given to the eleven is not separate from the mission of Jesus. When they baptize or administer any other sacrament, it is really the risen Jesus who is ministering and with whom they (and we) are cooperating. Jesus takes up this message in the final words of this brief discourse: 'And know [through contemplation] that I am with you always, to the end of time/the age/the world.'

The Ascension

In the concluding words, it is again a little preposition that is of great significance – here the word 'with'. This preposition is an expression of the theme of Matthew's gospel. In the annunciation of the birth of the Messiah we have the words of the angel to Joseph: 'His name will called Emmanuel, which means God-with-us' (Matthew 1:23).

'With' recurs in our Ascension scene today in the very last words of the gospel (28:20). This is the literary device of inclusion, common in ancient literature, in which what comes at the start and at the finish is an expression of what is important to all that comes between. Unique to Matthew is the saying of Jesus: 'Where two or three are gathered in my name, I shall be there with them' (Matthew 18:20)

At the climactic moment of all the gospels, the prayer of Jesus in Gethsemane, it is only in Matthew that Jesus asks the disciples to 'watch with me' (Matthew 26:36, 38, 40). This does not mean that Jesus was finding prayer on his own too difficult and badly needed their support. It means that the prayer he was expecting of them was to be in relationship and union with him. What were they asked to pray about? 'Pray that you do not come to the time of trial' are the words of Mark, of Matthew and of Luke.

In our prayer to Mary, to Jesus and to the Trinity, we may well take as an inspiration the words of the Preface of the feast of the Ascension: 'The Lord of all has passed beyond our sight, not to abandon us, but to be our hope.' I may simply profess in my own words what my hope is.

— 40 —

Come, Holy Spirit!

Then the disciples returned to Jerusalem from the mount called Olivet, which is near Jerusalem, a Sabbath day's journey away. When they had entered the city, they went to the upstairs room where they were staying, Peter, and John, and James, and Andrew, Philip and Thomas, Bartholomew and Matthew, James son of Alphaeus, and Simon the Zealot, and Judas the son of James. All these were constantly devoting themselves to prayer, together with certain women, including Mary the mother of Jesus, as well as his brothers.

When the day of Pentecost had come, they were all together in one place. And suddenly from heaven there came a sound like the rush of a violent wind, and it filled the entire house where they were sitting. Divided tongues, as of fire, appeared among them, and a tongue rested on each of them. All of them were filled with the Holy Spirit and began to speak in other languages, as the Spirit gave them ability.

Acts 1:12-15, 2 1-4

OUR PRAYER LIFE is an expression of the reality of our baptism. As such it is essentially a life of relationship with Father, Son and Holy Spirit. Generally, praying people readily relate to God as Father and to Jesus as Lord; but relationship to the Holy Spirit seems to raise special difficulty.

The main reason for this is that it is comparably easy for

us to have images of a Father figure or of a Son, or of the human Jesus who walked this earth; they readily engage our imagination, and after all it is imagination that is the key faculty in our normal human relationships. There are many wonderful spiritual statements about the Holy Spirit in Sacred Scripture, but the Spirit remains a disembodied person. That is why it can be a great help to praying about the Holy Spirit to start from a concrete human story like the above account of Luke in Acts of the early Christian community gathering to pray for the coming of God's Spirit, and then the actual event of Pentecost.

If we take up the text of Acts chapter one and two, it is not difficult for our imagination to become involved. We join the disciples on their journey back from the Ascension on Mt Olivet, and go with them to the upper room to pray. We may choose to focus on any favourites among the apostles who are named, and enter into conversation with them about the extraordinary events of these days and how they and we are affected by them.

Of course, we notice the presence of Mary among the group, and there is a lot to be gained by staying with her in prayer as she awaits the coming of the Holy Spirit; we may recall the words she heard at the Annunciation: 'The Holy Spirit will come upon you.'

Traditionally, the main prayer of Christians to the Holy Spirit is a prayer for the Spirit to come. There are the two great, ancient hymns, 'Come, Creator Spirit' from the tenth century, and 'Come, Holy Spirit', the Sequence at the Eucharist of Pentecost, from the 12th century. These are abbreviated into the fine, brief prayer: 'Come Holy Spirit and fill the hearts of your faithful and enkindle in them the fire of your love. Send forth your Spirit, O Lord, and they will be created, and you will renew the face of the earth.'

Already in these prayers, as in our reading from Acts, we have the wonderful image of fire to fill our imagining of the

Holy Spirit, that fire which cleanses by burning out evil, and prepares our hearts for new and greater life. We have, too, the image of tongues, which figures so prominently in the Pentecost story. We may well pause to pray that our tongue may give expression to something of divine Wisdom, rather than merely senseless chatter.

In Scripture there are countless images for the Holy Spirit; there is a feast for our imagination! The prime one amongst these is that of breath, from which the word Spirit derives. In Latin, *spiro* means 'I breathe'. The Holy Spirit is the breath of God, that breath God breathed into the earth God had formed to make Adam a living human being.

We sing in our hymn: 'Breathe on me, breath of God; fill me with life anew.' Every time we breathe we breathe in not only the air but God's Spirit. It can be a very contemplative act to focus on our breathing with this in mind. Nobody expresses this better than the incomparable John of the Cross:

> This breathing of the air is a gift which God will give a person in the communication of the Holy Spirit. By this divine breathing, the Holy Spirit elevates the heart sublimely and forms it and makes it capable of breathing God in the same breathing of love that the Father breathes in the Son and the Son in the Father. This breath of love is the Holy Spirit himself, who in the Father and the Son breathes out to the human heart in this transformation in order to unite it to himself. There would not be a true and total transformation if the heart were not transformed in the three persons of the most holy Trinity in an open and manifest degree. This kind of breathing of the Holy Spirit in the heart, by which God transforms it into Godself, is so sublime, delicate and deep a delight that the human tongue

finds it indescribable. Even what comes to pass in the communication given in this temporal transformation is unspeakable, for the heart united and transformed in God breathes out in God to God the very divine breathing that God breathes out in Godself to the person (*A Spiritual Canticle of the Soul and the Bridegroom Christ*, stanza 39:2).

Closely allied to breath is the image of wind, found here in our Pentecost story, and used by Jesus in speaking to Nicodemus to convey the image of the Holy Spirit. Once again it is not difficult to allow the experience of a breeze gently moving the leaves of a tree to fill our imagination with the presence of the Holy Spirit.

The Holy Spirit is the spirit of love and union, of peace and joy, of truth and freedom, of prayer and divine affiliation, of the Word of God, the spirit of God's indwelling and nearness to us. We have the great texts of the gifts of the Holy Spirit in Isaiah chapter 9, and in 1 Corinthians 12; and the fruit of the Spirit in Galatians chapter 5. Jesus promised to send the Holy Spirit as an Advocate and Comforter. Remember that the Holy Spirit has a twofold role in our lives: to comfort the afflicted and to afflict the comfortable.

— 41 —

Sacred Heart

At that time Jesus said, 'I thank you, Father, Lord of heaven and earth, because you have hidden these things from the wise and the intelligent and have revealed them to infants; yes, Father, for such was your gracious will. All things have been handed over to me by my Father, and no one knows the Father except the Son and anyone to whom the Son chooses to reveal him.

'Come to me, all you who are weary and are carrying heavy burdens, and I will give you rest. Take my yoke upon you and learn from me; for I am gentle and humble in heart, and you will find rest for your souls. For my yoke is easy and my burden is light.'

Matthew 11:25-30

THIS IS OUR GOSPEL READING for the Solemnity of the Sacred Heart, Year A. As we contemplate it, may it enlighten us to both the reality and the importance of this celebration for God's people. It is also the gospel for Year A of the 14th Sunday of Ordinary Time.

Devotion to the Sacred Heart, like many other popular devotions, and perhaps more so than most, has had a long and complex history in the life of God's People, the church.

At first glance it may seem odd that people would signal out parts of the human body of Jesus for special attention and devotion. The body part must always be understood in the context of the meaning conveyed by its symbolism. For instance, in his resurrection appearances Jesus drew the disciples' attention to his five wounds because they were a most powerful reminder and symbol of his sacrificial love in dying for them. As a result, devotion to the five wounds, especially to the spear wound in the side of Jesus had a prominent part in the spirituality of the early church. Many Fathers of the Church preached and wrote of that wound as being the fountain of the church's sacramental life. The heart, the wounded side, the love are intimately bound together.

The symbolic link between the human heart and love seems to be connatural to the human race. Countless expressions like 'I love you with all my heart' are a sure witness to this. In fact, the ceaseless repetition of 'heart' in romantic pop music has bombarded our minds almost to the point of being an obstacle to deeper and more spiritual appreciation of the symbolic link between the heart and authentic human love.

In the middle ages, the 13th century Saxon Benedictines, St Mechtilde and especially her follower St Gertrude the Great, had mystical experiences of the love of the heart of Jesus. The main flowering of the devotion to the Sacred Heart occurred in 17th century France. The spiritual theologian and founder of religious orders St John Eudes (1601-1680) was a forerunner in this field to the extraordinary private revelations of St Margaret Mary Alacoque (1647-1690). It is no coincidence that this happened in 17th century France, the home of the free-thinking philosophy called the Enlightenment. Authentic religion has both an intellectual life and an affective life. When the intellectual life of Catholicism was so severely threatened, the devotional life flourished.

For the next three centuries, devotion to the Sacred Heart became something of a touchstone of Catholic life. Religious congregations and lay sodalities under the name of Sacred Heart proliferated. In many countries every good Catholic family had a picture of the Sacred Heart on display in the home. Arising out of Margaret Mary's revelations, devotion to Mass on the first Friday of every month and devotion to the 'nine first Fridays' flourished.

Then came Vatican II. One of its outcomes was that a theologically better educated laity began to reject a lot of poor religious art and became more sceptical about private revelations, especially about taking too literally words heard coming from the mouth of Jesus or Mary. On both these counts devotion to the Sacred Heart was threatened. But there can be no threat to the love of Jesus for his people that the devotion has so well symbolized for centuries.

We begin our contemplation with our usual preparatory steps. Our gospel for the Solemnity of the Sacred Heart is one of the most powerful affective passages of Matthew's gospel. In a gospel dominated by great blocks of teaching, with Jesus often seeming like a new lawgiver going beyond the law of Moses, and a teacher to the Jews of ultimate reward and punishment, here he is speaking simply about the virtue of childlike simplicity, full of the joy of gratitude to the Father.

The first short paragraph of our gospel is a prayer of Jesus to the Father, so that we contemplate him here at prayer. Perhaps we join him in praying his words. Jesus thanks (blesses) the Father for hiding the mysteries of the kingdom (only accessible in contemplation) from the wise and intelligent (the scribes and Pharisees – the men of the law).

Then we have that beautiful line of filial love and devotion: 'Yes, Father, for such was your gracious will.' Matthew goes on to show that the gospel of John does not have a monopoly on presenting the intimacy of the relationship between Father and Son. His verse 27 is the same as John's great ending of his prologue: 'No one has ever seen God; it is the only Son who is into the heart of the Father who has revealed God' (John 1:18)

Jesus now turns to address the people, and us, in tender love and affection: 'Come to me, all who labour and are burdened, and I will give you rest. Shoulder my yoke [not a symbol of a burden or oppression, but of difficulties intimately shared]. Learn to be like me, meek and humble in heart.'

This last phrase gave us one of the two great aspirations to the Sacred Heart: 'Jesus meek and humble of heart, make my heart to be like yours.' In this age, when praying with a mantra has become a popular form of entry into deep contemplation, perhaps we can spend a prolonged time of prayer in repeating this aspiration over and over, together with the other great aspiration to the Sacred Heart: 'Heart of Jesus, burning with love for me, inflame my heart with love for you.'

It is the experience of praying people who have long used mantras such as these aspirations that, when they are tired or ill or when thoughts, feelings or awareness of God have simply dried up, the mantras seem to repeat themselves in their minds and hearts in a kind of apophatic contemplation – without using any images or ideas.

Our contemplation of this gospel of the Heart of Jesus may well lead us to spend a prolonged time in praying with one of these two mantras or praying over David Fleming's adaptation of the *Anima Christi*.

> Jesus, may all that is you flow into me.
> May your body and blood be my food and drink.
> May your passion and death be my strength and life.
> Jesus, with you by my side enough has been given.
> May the shelter I seek be the shadow of your cross.
> Let me not run from the love which you offer,
> But hold me safe from the forces of evil.
> On each of my dyings shed your light and your love.
> Keep calling me until that day comes,
> When, with your saints, I may praise you forever.
> Amen.

Appendix A

How Do I Contemplate a Gospel Mystery?

Preparatory steps for entering upon a time of contemplation.

1. It can be important to begin any time of contemplation slowly and thoughtfully, as outlined in the simple preparatory steps proposed by St Ignatius for any time of contemplation or meditation. This heightens our sense of alertness and awareness, our hope that the Lord will lead us into deeper union with him, and our desire to give our best in whole-hearted response to him.

2. It is usually helpful to be prepared ahead of the time of prayer by knowing where, when and with what material I am going to pray.

3. I move slowly towards the place for my prayer, and stop a few paces away. An exercise of relaxation and awareness is usually very helpful. A few minutes of attention to one's breathing can be a great help.

4. Next I make the preparatory prayer: 'Lord, I ask for the grace that all that I am and all I do may be directed purely to your service and praise.'

5. As I begin, I spend a few moments remembering again the subject matter for my coming contemplation.

6. I remember what grace I desire to receive in this time of contemplation. When contemplating a gospel Mystery, it will always be to know our Lord better, to love him more fully, and to follow him more closely.

How Do I Contemplate a Gospel Mystery?

7. It is recommended that we repeat steps 2-6 whenever we enter a time of contemplation of one of the mysteries.

Concluding Prayers

It is normal practice to conclude a time of conversation (dialogue, colloquy) with a formal prayer:

Conversation with Mary: a Hail Mary.

Conversation with Jesus: Perhaps one or both of the aspirations to the Sacred Heart:

> 'Heart of Jesus, burning with love for me, inflame my heart with love for you.'

> 'Jesus, meek and humble of heart, make my heart to be like yours.'

Or:

> 'Lord I am not worthy to receive you. Only say the word and I will be healed.'

Or the *Anima Christi*. Here is the modem rendition of David Fleming SJ:

> Jesus, may all that is you flow into me.
> May your body and blood be my food and drink.
> May your passion and death be my strength and life.
> Jesus, with you by my side enough has been given.
> May the shelter I seek be the shadow of your cross.
> Let me not run from the love which you offer,
> But hold me safe from the forces of evil.
> On each of my dyings shed your light and your love.
> Keep calling me until that day comes,
> When, with your saints, I may praise you forever.
> Amen.

COME, LORD JESUS

Models for Contemplation of the Mysteries of the Lord.*

101. FIRST DAY AND FIRST CONTEMPLATION

This is a contemplation on the Incarnation. After the preparatory prayer and three preludes there are three points and a colloquy

Prayer. The usual preparatory prayer.

102. First Prelude. This will consist in calling to mind the history of the subject I have to contemplate. Here it will be how the Three Divine Persons look down upon the whole expanse or circuit of all the earth, filled with human beings. Since they see that all are going down to hell, they decree in their eternity that the Second Person should become human to save the human race. So when the fullness of time had come, they sent the Angel Gabriel to our Lady.

103. Second Prelude. This is a mental representation of the place. It will be here to see the great extent of the surface of the earth, inhabited by so many different peoples, and especially to see the house and room of our Lady in the city of Nazareth in the province of Galilee.

104. Third Prelude. This is to ask for what I desire. Here it will be to ask for an intimate knowledge of our Lord, who has become a man for me, that I may love him more and follow him more closely.

106. First Point. This will be to see the different persons:

First, those on the face of the earth, in such great diversity in dress and in manner of acting. Some are white, some black; some at peace, and some at war; some weeping, some laughing; some

---

* Taken from the classic translation of the *Spiritual Exercises of St Ignatius*, translated by Louis Puhl SJ [1951], current edition available from Loyola Press, Chicago, USA.

well, some sick; some coming into the world, and some dying; and so on...

Second, I will see and consider the Three Divine Persons seated on the royal dais or throne of the Divine Majesty. They look down upon the whole surface of the earth, and behold all nations in great blindness, going down to death while desperately in need of salvation.

Third, I will see our Lady and the angel saluting her. I will reflect upon this to draw profit from what I see.

107. Second Point. This will be to listen to what the persons on the face of the earth say, that is, how they speak to one another, swear and blaspheme, etc. I will also hear what the Divine Persons say, that is, 'Let us work the redemption of the human race', etc. Then I will listen to what the angel and our Lady say. Finally, I will reflect upon all I hear to draw profit from their words.

108. Third Point. This will be to consider what the persons on the face of the earth do, for example, wound, kill and die. Also what the Divine Persons do, namely, work the most holy Incarnation, etc. Likewise, what the angel and our Lady do; how the angel carries out his office of divine ambassador; and how our Lady humbles herself, and offers thanks to the Divine Majesty. Then I shall reflect upon all to draw some fruit from each of these details.

109. Colloquy. The exercise should be closed with a colloquy. I will think over what I ought to say to the Three Divine Persons, to the eternal Word incarnate, or to his Mother, our Lady. According to the light that I have received, I will beg for grace to follow and imitate more closely our Lord, who has just become a man for me.

Close with an Our Father.

110. THE SECOND CONTEMPLATION
The Nativity

Prayer. The usual preparatory prayer.

111. First Prelude. This is the history of the mystery. Here it will be that our Lady, about nine months with child, and, as may be piously believed, seated on an ass, set out from Nazareth. She was accompanied by Joseph and a maid, who was leading an ox. They are going to Bethlehem to pay the tribute that Caesar imposed on those lands.

112. Second Prelude. This is a mental representation of the place. It will consist here in seeing in imagination the way from Nazareth to Bethlehem. Consider its length, its breadth; whether level, or through valleys and over hills. Observe also the place or cave where Christ is born; whether big or little; whether high or low; and how it is arranged.

113. Third Prelude. This will be the same as in the preceding contemplation and identical in form with it.

114. First Point. This will consist in seeing the persons, namely, our Lady, St Joseph, and the Child Jesus after his birth. I will make myself a poor little unworthy slave, and, as though present, look upon them, contemplate them, and serve them in their needs with all possible homage and reverence. Then I will reflect on myself that I may reap some fruit.

115. Second Point. This is to consider, observe, and contemplate what the persons are saying, and then to reflect on myself and draw some fruit from it.

116. Third Point. This will be to see and consider what they are doing, for example, making the journey and labouring that our Lord might be born in extreme poverty, and that after many labours,

after hunger, thirst, heat and cold, after insults and outrages, He might die on the cross, and all this for me. Then I will reflect and draw some spiritual fruit from what I have seen.

117. Colloquy. Close with a colloquy as in the preceding contemplation, and with the Lord's Prayer.

118. THE THIRD CONTEMPLATION

This will be a repetition of the first and second exercises

After the preparatory prayer and the three preludes, a repetition of the First and Second Exercises will be made. In doing this, attention should always be given to some more important parts in which one has experienced understanding, consolation, or desolation. Close the exercise with a colloquy and the Lord's Prayer.

119. In this repetition and in all those which follow, the same order of proceeding should be observed as in the repetitions of the First Week. The subject matter is changed but the same form is observed.

120. THE FOURTH CONTEMPLATION

This will consist in applying the five senses to the matter of the first and second contemplations.

After the preparatory prayer and the three preludes, it will be profitable with the aid of the imagination to apply the five senses to the subject matter of the First and Second Contemplation in the following manner:

122. First Point. This consists in seeing in imagination the persons, and in contemplating and meditating in detail the circumstances in which they are, and then in drawing some fruit from what has been seen.

123. Second Point. This is to hear what they are saying, or what they might say, and then by reflecting on oneself to draw some profit from what has been heard.

124. Third Point. This is to smell the infinite fragrance, and taste the infinite sweetness of the divinity. Likewise to apply these senses to the soul and its virtues, and to all according to the person we are contemplating, and to draw fruit from this.

125. Fourth Point. This is to apply the sense of touch, for example, by embracing and kissing the place where the persons stand or are seated, always taking care to draw some fruit from this.

126. Colloquy. Conclude with a colloquy and with the Lord's Prayer as in the First and Second Contemplations.

Appendix B

Contemplative Prayer*

2709 What is contemplative Prayer? St Teresa answers, 'Contemplative prayer (*oracion mental*) in my opinion is nothing else than a close sharing between friends; it means taking time frequently to be alone with him who we know loves us.'[1]

Contemplative prayer seeks him 'whom my soul loves'.[2] It is Jesus, and in him the Father. We seek him, because to desire him is always the beginning of love, and we seek him in that pure faith which causes us to be born of him and to live in him. In this inner prayer we can still meditate, but our attention is fixed on the Lord himself.

2710 The choice of the time and duration of the prayer arises from a determined will, revealing the secrets of the heart. One does not undertake contemplative prayer only when one has the time: one makes time for the Lord, with the firm determination not to give up, no matter what trials and dryness one may encounter. One cannot always meditate, but one can always enter into inner prayer, independently of the conditions of health, work, or emotional state. The heart is the place of this quest and encounter, in poverty and in faith.

2711 Entering into contemplative prayer is like entering into the Eucharistic liturgy. We 'gather up' the heart, recollect our whole being under the prompting of the Holy Spirit, abide in the dwelling place of the Lord which we are, awaken our faith in

---

*From the *Catechism of the Catholic Church*, Part 4, Section 1, Chapter 3.

order to enter into the presence of him who awaits us. We let our masks fall and turn our hearts back to the Lord who loves us, so as to hand ourselves over to him as an offering to be purified and transformed.

2712 Contemplative prayer is the prayer of the child of God, and of the forgiven sinner who agrees to welcome the love by which he is loved and who wants to respond by loving even more.[3] But he knows that the love he is returning is poured out by the Spirit in his heart, for everything is grace from God. Contemplative prayer is the poor and humble surrender to the loving will of the Father in ever deeper union with his beloved Son.

2713 Contemplative prayer is the simplest expression of the mystery of prayer. It is a gift, a grace; it can be accepted only in humility and poverty. Contemplative prayer is a covenant relationship established by God within our hearts.[4] Contemplative prayer is a communion in which the Holy Trinity conforms humanity, the image of God, 'to their likeness'.

2714 Contemplative prayer is also the pre-eminently intense time of prayer. In it the Father strengthens our inner being with power through his Spirit, 'that Christ may dwell in [our] hearts through faith' and we may be 'grounded in love'.[5]

2715 Contemplation is a gaze of faith, fixed on Jesus. 'I look at him and he looks at me.' This is what a certain peasant of Ars said to his holy curé about his prayer before the tabernacle. This focus on Jesus is a renunciation of self. His gaze purifies our hearts; the light of the countenance of Jesus illumines the eyes of our hearts and teaches us to see everything in the light of his truth and his compassion for all men. Contemplation also turns its gaze on the mysteries of the life of Christ. Thus it learns the 'interior knowledge of our Lord', the more to love him and follow him.[6]

Contemplative Prayer

2716 Contemplative prayer is hearing the Word of God. Far from being passive, such attentiveness is the obedience of faith, the unconditional acceptance of a servant, and the loving commitment of a child. It participates in the 'Yes' of the Son become servant and the *Fiat* of God's lowly handmaid.

2717 Contemplative prayer is silence, the 'symbol of the world to come,'[7] or 'silent love'.[8] Words in this kind of prayer are not speeches; they are like kindling that feeds the fire of love. In this silence, unbearable to the 'outer' man, the Father speaks to us his incarnate Word, who suffered, died, and rose; in this silence the Spirit of adoption enables us to share in the prayer of Jesus.

2718 Contemplative prayer is union with the prayer of Christ in so far as it makes us participate in his mystery. The mystery of Christ is celebrated in the church in the Eucharist, and the Holy Spirit makes it come alive in contemplative prayer so that our charity will manifest it in our acts.

2719 Contemplative prayer is a communion of love bearing Life for the multitude, to the extent that it consents to abide in the night of faith. The Paschal night of the Resurrection passes through the night of the agony and the tomb – the three intense moments of the Hour of Jesus which his Spirit (and not 'the flesh [which] is weak') brings to life in prayer. We must be willing to 'keep watch with him one hour'.[9]

In brief

2724 Contemplative prayer is the simple expression of the mystery of prayer. It is a gaze of faith fixed on Jesus, an attentiveness to the Word of God, a silent love. It achieves real union with the prayer of Christ to the extent that it makes us share in his mystery.

Notes

1. St Teresa of Jesus, *The Book of Her Life*, 8, 5, in *The Collected works of St Teresa of Avila*, tr. K. Kavanaugh OCD, & O. Rodriguez OCD (Washington DC: Institute of Carmelite Studies, 1976), 1, 67.

2. Song 1:7; see 3:1-4.

3. See Luke 7:36-50; 19:1-10.

4. See Jeremiah 31:33.

5. Ephesians 3:16-17.

6. St Ignatius of Loyola, *Spiritual Exercises*, 104.

7. St Isaac of Nineveh, *Tract. myst.*, 66.

8. St John of the Cross, *Maxims and Counsels*, 53, in *The Collected Works of St John of the Cross*, tr. K. Kavanaugh OCD & O. Rodriguez OCD (Washington DC: Institute of Carmelite Studies, 1979), 678.

9. See Matthew 26:40.

Appendix C

Excerpts from the *Spiritual Journal* of St Ignatius

These short readings are taken from the *Spiritual Journal* of St Ignatius for a three week period, 8-28 February 1544.

Mass of the Holy Name of Jesus
7. Friday [8 February]

After Mass, devotion not without tears, while I considered the choices in the election for an hour and a half or more. When I came to offer what seemed to me most reasonable, and to which my will most impelled, viz. that no fixed income should be allowed, I desired make this offering to the Father through the mediation and the prayers of the Mother and the Son. First, I prayed her to assist me before her Son and the Father. Next I implored the Son that together with the Mother he might help me before the Father. Then I felt within me that I approached, or was taken before, the Father, and with this movement my hair rose and I felt what seemed a very remarkable burning in every part of my body, followed by tears and the most intense devotion.

Mass of the Holy Spirit
10. Monday [11 February]

During my customary prayer, without reconsidering the reasons for poverty, I offered it to God Our Lord or implored Him that the offering already made might be accepted by His Divine Majesty; I felt considerable devotion and tears. A little later I made a colloquy with the Holy Spirit, in preparation for saying His Mass; I experienced the same devotion and tears, and seemed to see or feel Him in a dense clarity or in the colour of a burning flame – a way quite strange to me – all of which confirmed me in my election.

Later, in preparation for considering and going into the various choices, now my mind was made up, I took out the written pros and cons to consider them. I prayed to Our Lady, then to the Son, and to the Father, that He might give me his Spirit to assist me in my reasonings and to give me clarity of mind, even though I spoke of the matter as already settled. I felt considerable devotion and certain very clear-sighted intuitions. Thus I sat down considering almost in general whether the income should be complete, partial, or not at all. Then I began to lose the desire to look into pros and cons and at the same moment I received new insights, viz. that the Son first sent his Apostles to preach in poverty, and later the Holy Spirit, by granting his spirit and his gift of tongues, confirmed them, and thus, since both Father and Son sent the Holy Spirit, all three Persons confirmed such a mission.

Mass of Our Lady
12. Wednesday [13 February]

I knew that I was gravely at fault in having left the Divine Persons on the previous day during the thanksgiving: I wanted to abstain from celebrating the Mass of the Trinity that I thought of saying, and take as my intercessors the Mother and the Son, that my fault might be forgiven me and I myself restored to my former grace; I would keep away from three Divine Persons and so not apply myself immediately to them for the former graces and offerings: I would not say their Masses all that week, mortifying myself by thus absenting myself. Then I experienced very great devotion, and most intense tears, not only during prayer but while I vested; I sobbed and as I could feel the Mother and the Son to be interceding for me, I felt a complete security that the Eternal Father would restore me to my former state. Later, before, during and after Mass, greatly increased devotion and a great abundance of tears: I saw and felt the mediators: I was most sure I would regain what was lost.

Mass of Our Lady in the Temple. Simeon.
14. Friday [15 February]

During my first prayer, when I named the Eternal Father, etc., there came a feeling of internal sweetness that continued, not without an impulse to weep: later considerable devotion, and, towards the end, much greater still; no mediators or persons revealed themselves. Next, on preparing to leave for Mass, as I began to pray, I could feel, and was shown, Our Lady, also how great had been my fault the previous day: I felt moved within and wept, for I seemed to be putting Our Lady to shame in having her intercede for me so often because of my many failings. So much so that Our Lady hid from me and I found no devotion in her or higher than her. A little later, when I sought to go higher, as I could not find Our Lady, a mighty impulse to weep and sob gripped me and I seemed to see or feel that the Heavenly Father showed Himself propitious and kind – to the point of making clear to me that he would be pleased if Our Lady, whom I could not see, would intercede.

While preparing the altar, after I had vested, and during Mass, I experienced greater interior impulses and wept very copiously and intensely, sobbing violently. Often I could not speak. The same continued after Mass. During much of this time, before, during and after mass, I felt and saw clearly that Our Lady was very propitious, pleading before the Father. Indeed during the prayers to the Father and the Son, and at His consecration I could not but feel or see her, as though she were part or rather portal of the great grace that I could feel in my spirit. (at the consecration she showed that her own flesh was in that of her Son) with so many intuitions that they could not be written. No doubts about the first offering that was made.

Mass of the Trinity and End

Later I decided to rise and thought of delaying the dinner hour and taking measures to ensure that I should not be disturbed until I found the grace I desired; I then felt new warmth and a devotion that made me weep. While dressing I thought of abstaining for three days in order to find what I desired. When the realization dawned on me that even this thought was from God, new strength, warmth and spiritual devotion filled me, impelling me ever more to weep. A little later I wondered where I should begin and it occurred to me that it might be with all the Saints, putting my cause in their hands, so that they might pray to Our Lady and her Son to be intercessors on my behalf before the Blessed Trinity. With great devotion and intensity of feeling, I felt my face streaming with tears; in this state I went for confirmation of the past offerings, including many things in my colloquy – beseeching and nominating as intercessors on my behalf the Angels, the holy Fathers, the Apostles and Disciples and all the Saints, etc., that they might plead to Our Lady and her Son: then I started once more to beseech Our Lady and her Son with long reasonings that my concluded confirmation and thanksgiving might rise before the throne of the Blessed Trinity. During all this and from then onwards, a great flood of tears, and many impulses and interior sobs. It seemed moreover as if each vein and part of my body was making itself sensibly felt. Before their entire Heavenly Court I made the concluded confirmation of my offering to the Blessed Trinity, giving thanks with great and intense affection, first to the Divine Persons, then to Our Lady and her Son, then passing through the Angels, the holy Fathers, the Apostles, Disciples, to all the Saints, men and women, and to all persons who had helped me to do this. Later while I prepared the altar and vested, there came to me: 'Eternal Father, confirm me'; 'Eternal Son, confirm me'; 'Eternal Holy Spirit, confirm me'; 'Holy Trinity, confirm me';

'My One Sole God, confirm me'. I repeated this many times with great force, devotion and tears, and very deeply did I feel it. And when I asked once, 'Eternal Father, will you not confirm me?', I knew He would: so also with Son and Holy Spirit.

Mass of the day
23. Sunday [24 February]
During the customary prayer, from the beginning to the end inclusive, I was helped by grace very far inside and gentle, full of devotion, warm and very sweet. While preparing the altar and vesting, the name of Jesus was shown me: I felt great love, confirmation and an increased resolve to follow Him. I wept and sobbed, throughout Mass, great devotion and many tears; the devotion and tears had Jesus as their object [Confirmation of Jesus].

I could not turn myself to the other Persons, except in so far as the First Person was Father of such a Son: then I began to exclaim spiritually, 'How He is Father, and how He is Son!' During the prayer after Mass I had the same feeling towards the Son. I had desired the confirmation by the Blessed Trinity, and now I felt it was communicated to me through Jesus. He showed Himself to me and gave me great interior strength and a sense of security that the confirmation was granted. I did not fear for the future. So it occurred to me, and I at once complied, to pray to Jesus to obtain pardon for me from the Blessed Trinity. I felt an increase of devotion, tears and sobs, and the hope of obtaining the grace – for I was quite resolute and strengthened for the future. Later, when I moved nearer to the fire, I once more was shown Jesus and felt great devotion and the impulse to weep.

Later, when I walked in the street, I was shown Him and felt very great impulses with tears. After I had spoken to Carpi, on my way back, the same happened and I felt great devotion. After the midday meal, especially after I passed through the door of the Vicar Bishop, in the house of Trani, I felt or saw Jesus, and experienced great interior impulses and wept much. I begged and implored Jesus to obtain my pardon from the Blessed Trinity; I found there remained with me great confidence for the success of my prayer. On these occasions my love was so great, I so felt and saw Jesus, that it seemed that nothing could happen in the future capable of separating me from Him or of making me doubt about the graces and confirmation I had received.

Mass for the first day of Lent
26. Wednesday [27 February]

When I write this, my understanding feels drawn to see the Blessed Trinity, and appears to see, although distinctly as before, three Persons. During Mass, when I said the prayer that begins, '*Domine, Jesu Christe, Fili Dei* Vivi ...', etc., it seemed to me in spirit that whereas before I had seen Jesus, as I said, then what I saw was white, that is His humanity, on this occasion my feeling in my soul was different, i.e., I was aware not of the humanity alone, but of Jesus being completely my God, etc., with a fresh flood of tears and great devotion, etc.

Mass of the Trinity. No. 7
27. Thursday [28 February]

Great devotion during the customary prayer: helped by great grace full of warmth, light and love. On entering the chapel, new devotion: when I knelt, Jesus was disclosed to me ... or I saw him ... at the foot of the Blessed Trinity: at that, new impulses and tears. This vision did not last as long, nor was it as clear as that of Wednesday although it seemed of the same type.

Appendix D
A Letter on the Interior Life*

1. Prologue

BROTHER GUIGO to his dear brother Gervase:

Rejoice in the Lord. I owe you a debt of love, brother, because you began to love me first; and, since in your previous letter you have invited me to write to you, I feel bound to reply. So I decided to send you my thoughts on the spiritual exercises proper to cloistered monks, so that you who have come to know more about these matters by your experience than I have by theorising about them may pass judgment on my thoughts and amend them. And it is fitting that I should offer these first results of our work together to you before anyone else, so that you may gather the first fruits of the young tree (Psalm 144:12) which by praiseworthy stealth you extracted from the bondage of Pharaoh (Exodus 13:14), where it was tended alone, and set it in its place amongst the ordered rows (Canticles 6:3-9), once you had grafted on to the stock like a good nurseryman the branch skilfully cut from the wild olive.

2. The four rungs of the ladder

One day when I was busy working with my hands I began to think about our spiritual work, and all at once four stages in our spiritual work came into my mind – reading, meditation, prayer and contemplation. These make a ladder for monks by which they may rise from earth to heaven: it has few rungs, yet its length is immense

---

*Also called 'The Ladder of Monks', *Scala Claustralium*, by 12th century Carthusian monk, Guigo II (Guy the Angelic), and considered the first description of methodical prayer in the western tradition.)

and wonderful, for its lower end rests upon the earth, but its top pierces the clouds and touches heavenly secrets (Genesis 28:12). Just as its rungs or degrees have different names or numbers, they differ also in order and quality; and if anyone enquires carefully into their properties and functions, what each one does in relation to us, the differences between them and their order of importance, he will consider whatever trouble and care he may spend on this little and easy in comparison with the help and consolation he gains.

Reading is the careful study of the scriptures, concentrating all one's powers on it. Meditation is the busy application of the mind to seek with the help of one's own reason for knowledge of hidden truth. Prayer is the heart's devoted turning to God to do away evil and obtain what is good. Contemplation is when the mind is in some sort lifted up to God and held above itself, so that it tastes the joys of everlasting sweetness. Now that we have described the four degrees, we must see what their functions are in relation to us.

3. The functions of these degrees

Reading seeks for the sweetness of a blessed life, meditation perceives it, prayer asks for it, contemplation tastes it. Reading as it were puts the food whole into the mouth, meditation chews it and breaks it up, prayer extracts its flavour, contemplation is the sweetness itself which gladdens and refreshes. Reading works on the outside, meditation on the pith: prayer asks for what we long for, contemplation gives us delight in the sweetness which we have found. To make this clearer let us take one of the many possible examples.

4. The function of reading

I hear the words read: 'Blessed are the pure in heart, for they shall see God' (Matthew 5:8). This is a short text of scripture, but it is of great sweetness, like a grape that is put into the mouth, filled with many senses to feed the soul; and when the soul has carefully examined it, it says to itself, 'There may be something good here: I shall search my heart and try to understand and find this purity, for this is indeed a precious and desirable thing, when those who have it are called blessed, and it has for its reward the vision of God which is eternal life, and it is praised in so many places in sacred scripture.' So, wishing to have a fuller understanding of this, the soul begins to bite and chew upon this grape, as though putting it in a wine press while it stirs up its powers of reasoning to ask what this precious purity may be and how it may be had.

5. The function of meditation

When meditation busily applies itself to this work, it does not remain on the outside, it is not detained by unimportant things, it climbs higher, it goes to the heart of the matter, it examines each point thoroughly. It takes careful note that the text does not say, 'Blessed are the pure in body', but 'the pure in heart'; for it is not enough to have hands clean from evil deeds (Genesis 37:22), unless our minds are cleansed from impure thoughts; and we have the authority of the prophet for this, when he says, "Who shall climb the mountain of the Lord, and who shall stand in his holy place? He whose hands are guiltless and whose heart is pure' (Psalm 43:3-4).

And meditation perceives how greatly that same prophet seeks for this purity of heart when he prays, 'Create a pure heart in me, God' (Psalm 51:10), and in another place, 'If I know that there is wickedness in my heart, the Lord will not hear me' (Psalm 66:18). It thinks what care the saintly man Job took to preserve this purity when he said, 'I have made a pact with my eyes, so that I would not think about any maid' (Job 31:1). See how this holy man guarded himself, who shut his eyes lest he should look upon vain things (Psalm 119:37), lest he should perhaps unguardedly see that which afterwards he should long for despite himself.

After meditation has so pondered upon purity of heart, it begins to think of the reward, of how glorious and joyful it would be to see the face of the Lord so greatly longed for, 'fairer than all the sons of men' (Psalm 45:2), no longer rejected and wretched (see Isaiah 53:2), nor with that earthly beauty with which his mother clothed him, but wearing the robe of immortality and crowned with the diadem (Sirach 6:32) which his Father bestowed upon him on the day of his resurrection and glory, the day 'which the Lord has made' (Psalm 118:24). It thinks how this vision will bring it the fullness of what the prophet says, 'I shall be filled when your glory appears' (Psalm 17:15).

Do you see how much juice has come from one little grape, how great a fire has been kindled from a spark, how this small piece of metal – 'Blessed are the pure in heart, for they shall see God' – has acquired a new dimension by being hammered out on the anvil of meditation? And even more might be drawn from it at the hands of someone really expert. I feel that 'the well is deep', but I am still an ignorant beginner, and it is only with difficulty that I have found something in which to draw up these few drops (John 4:11).

When the soul is set alight by this kindling, and when its flames are fanned by these desires, it receives a first intimation of the sweetness, not yet by tasting but through its sense of smell, when the alabaster box is broken (Mark 14:3); and from this it deduces how sweet it would be to be so full of joy. But what is it to do? It is consumed with longing, yet it can find no means of its own to have what it longs for; and the more it searches the more it thirsts ... As long as it is meditating, so long is its suffering, because it does not feel that sweetness which, as meditation shows, belongs to purity of heart, but which it does not give.

A man will not experience this sweetness whilst reading or meditating, 'unless it happened to be given to him from above' (John 19:11). The good and the wicked alike can read and meditate; and even pagan philosophers by the use of reason discovered the highest and truest good. But 'although they knew God, they did not glorify him as God' (Romans 1:21), and trusting in their own powers they said, 'Let us sing our own praises, our words are our own' (Psalm 12:5). They had not the grace to understand what they had the ability to see. 'They perished in their own ideas' (Romans 1:21), and 'all their wisdom was swallowed up' (Psalm 107:27), that wisdom to which the study of human learning had led them, not the Spirit of wisdom who alone grants true wisdom, that sweet-tasting knowledge which rejoices and refreshes the soul in which it dwells with a sweetness beyond telling; and of this wisdom it is said, 'Wisdom will not enter a disaffected soul (Wisdom 1:4)

This wisdom comes only from God: and just as the Lord entrusted the office of baptizing to many, but reserved to himself the power and authority truly to remit sins in baptism, so that John called him by his office and defined it when he said 'This is he who baptizes (John 1:33), so we may say of him, 'This is he who gives the sweetness of wisdom and makes knowledge sweet to the soul. He gives words to many, but to few that wisdom of the soul which the Lord apportions to whom he pleases and when he pleases (1 Corinthians 12:11).

6. The function of prayer

So the soul, seeing that by itself it cannot attain to that sweetness of knowing and feeling for which it longs, and that the more the heart abases itself, the more God is exalted, humbles itself and betakes itself to prayer, saying, 'Lord, you are not seen except by the pure of heart: I seek by reading and meditating what is true purity of heart and how it may be had, so that, with its help I may know you, if only a little. Lord, for long have I meditated in my heart (Psalm 77:6), seeking to see your face. It is the sight of you, Lord, that I have sought; and all the while in my meditation the fire of longing (Psalm 39:4), the desire to know you more fully, has increased.

When you break for me the bread of sacred scripture (Luke 24 30-31), you have shown yourself to me in that breaking of bread, and the more I see you, the more I long to see you, no more from without, in the rind of the letter, but within in the letter's hidden meaning. Nor do I ask this, Lord, because of my own merits, but because of your mercy. I too in my unworthiness confess my sins with the woman who said that 'even the little dogs eat of the fragments that fall from the table of their masters' (Matthew 15:27). So give me, Lord, some pledge of what I hope to inherit, at least one drop of heavenly rain with which to refresh my thirst (Luke 16:24), for I am on fire with love (Canticles 2:5).

7. The effects of contemplation

So the soul by such burning words inflames its own desire, makes known its state, and by such spells it seeks to call its spouse. But the Lord, whose eyes are upon the just, and whose ears can catch not only the words (Psalm 34:19; 1 Peter 3:12), but the very meaning of their prayers, does not wait until the longing soul has said all its say, but breaks in upon the middle of its prayer, runs to meet it in all haste, sprinkled with heavenly dew, anointed with the most precious perfumes; and he restores the weary soul, he slakes its thirst, he feeds its hunger, he makes the soul forget all earthly things; by making it die to itself he gives it new life, in a wonderful way, and by making it drunk he brings it back to its true senses.

And, just as in the performance of some bodily functions the soul is so conquered by carnal desire that it loses all use of the reason, and man becomes as it were wholly carnal, so on the contrary in this exalted contemplation all carnal motions are so conquered and drawn out of the soul that in no way is the flesh opposed to the spirit, and man becomes as it were wholly spiritual.

8. The signs of the coming of grace

But, Lord, how are we to know you do this, what will be the sign of your coming? Can it be that the heralds and witnesses of this consolation and joy are sighs and tears? If it is so, then the word consolation is being used in a completely new sense, the reverse of its ordinary connotation. What has consolation in common with sighs, joy with tears, if indeed these are to be called tears and not rather an abundance of spiritual dew, poured from above and overflowing, an outward purification as a sign of inward cleansing? For just as in the baptism of infants by the outward washing the inward cleansing is typified and shown, here conversely an outward washing proceeds from the inner cleansing.

These are blessed tears, by which our inward stains are cleansed, by which the fires of our sins are put out. 'Blessed are they who weep so, for they shall rejoice' (Matthew 5:5). When you weep so, O my soul, recognize your spouse, embrace him whom you long for, make yourself drunk with this torrent of delight (Psalm 36:8) and suck the honey and milk of consolation from the breast (Isaiah 66:11). The wonderful rewards and comforts which your spouse has brought and awarded you are sobbings and tears. These tears are the generous draught which he gives you to drink (Psalm 80, 5). Let these tears be your bread by day and night (Psalm 42:4), the bread which strengthens the heart of man (Psalm 104:15), sweeter than honey and the honeycomb (Psalm 19:10).

O Lord Jesu, if these tears, provoked by thinking of you and longing for you, are sweet, how sweet will be the joy which we shall have to see you face to face? If it is so sweet to weep for you, how sweet will it be to rejoice in you? But why do we give this public utterance to what should be said in secret? Why do we try to express in everyday language affections which no language can describe? Those who have not known such things do not understand them, for they could learn more clearly of them only from the book of experience where God's grace itself is the teacher (1 John 2:27). Otherwise it is of no use for the reader to search in earthly books: there is little sweetness in the study of the literal sense, unless there be a commentary, which is found in the heart, to reveal the inward sense.

9. How grace is hidden

O my soul, we have talked about this too long. Yet it would have been good for us to be here, to look with Peter and John upon the glory of the spouse and to remain a while with him, had it been his will that we should make here not two, not three tabernacles (Matthew 17:4), but one in which we might all dwell, and be filled with joy. But now the spouse says, 'Let me go, for now the dawn is coming up' (Genesis 32:26), now you have received the light of grace and the visitation which you asked for. So he gives his blessing and withers the nerve of the thigh, and changes Jacob's name to Israel (Genesis 32:25-32), and then for a little while he withdraws, this spouse waited for so long, so soon gone again. He goes, it is true, for this visitation ends, and with the sweetness of contemplation; but yet he stays, for he guides us, he gives us grace, he joins us to himself.

10. How, when grace is hidden for a time, it works in us for good

But do not fear, O bride of the spouse, do not despair, do not think yourself despised, if for a little while he turns his face away from you. These things all work together for your good (Romans 8:28), and you profit from his coming and from his withdrawal. He comes to you and then he goes away again: he comes for your consolation, he goes away to put you on your guard, for fear that too much consolation should puff you up (2 Corinthians 12:7), and that you, having the spouse always with you, should begin to despise your brethren, and to attribute this consolation not to his grace, but to your natural powers. For this grace the spouse bestows when he pleases and to whom he pleases: it is not possessed as though by lawful title.

There is a common saying that too much familiarity breeds contempt: and so he withdraws himself so that he is not despised for being too attentive, so that when he is absent he may be desired the more, that being desired he may be sought more eagerly, that having long been sought for, he may at last be found with greater thankfulness. Then, too, if we never lacked this consolation, which is a mere shadow and fraction (1 Corinthians 13:12) in comparison with the future glory which will be shown us (Romans 8:18), we might think that we have here on earth our eternal home, and so we should seek less for our life in eternity (Hebrews 13:14).

So, therefore, lest we should consider this present exile our true home, this pleasure our whole reward, the spouse comes and withdraws by turn, now bringing us consolation, now exchanging all this for weakness (Psalm 41:4). For a short time he allows us to taste how sweet he is (Psalm 34:8), and before our taste is satisfied he withdraws; and it is in this way, by flying above us with wings outspread, that he encourages us to fly (Deuteronomy 32:11), and says in effect: See now you have a little taste of how sweet and delightful I am (1 Peter 2:3), but if you wish to have your fill of this sweetness, hasten after me drawn by my sweet-smelling perfumes (Canticles 1:3), lift up your heart to where I am at the right hand of God the Father (Acts 6:55). There you will see me (John 16:19) not darkly in a mirror but face to face (1 Corinthians 13:12), and your heart's joy will be complete, and no-one shall take this joy away from you (John 16:22).

11. How much the soul must be on its guard after it has been visited by grace

But take care, bride of the spouse: when he goes away, he does not go far; and even if you cannot see him, you are always in his sight. He is full of eyes in front and behind (Ezekiel 1:18), you cannot hide from him anywhere, for he surrounds you with those messengers of his, spirits who serve to bring back shrewd reports, to watch how you behave when he is not there, to denounce you to him if they detect in you any marks of wantonness and vileness. This is a jealous spouse (Exodus 34:14): he will leave you at once and give his favours to others if you play him false with anyone, trying to please anyone more than him. This spouse is fastidious, he is of gentle birth, he is rich, 'he is fairer than all the sons of men' (Esra 45:2), and so he will not deign to take a bride who is not fair. If he sees in you any blemish, any wrinkle (Ephesians 5:27), he will at once turn away from you (Isaiah 1:15). He cannot bear uncleanness of any kind. So be chaste, be truly modest and meek, if you wish often to enjoy your spouse's company.

I am afraid that I have talked too long of this to you, but I have been compelled to it by the abundance and the sweetness of my material: I have not deliberately drawn it out, but its very sweetness has drawn it out of me against my will.

12. Recapitulation

Let us now gather together by way of summary what we have already said at length, so that we may have a better view by looking at it altogether. You can see from what has already been said by way of examples, how these degrees are joined to each other. One precedes another, not only in the order of time, but of causality.

Reading comes first, and is as it were the foundation; it provides the subject matter which we must use for meditation. Meditation considers more carefully what is to be sought after; it digs (Proverbs 2:4), as it were, for treasure which it finds (Matthew 13:44) and reveals, but since it is not in meditation's power to seize upon the treasure, it directs us to prayer.

Prayer lifts itself up to God with all its strength, and begs for the treasure which it longs for, which is the sweetness of contemplation. Contemplation when it comes rewards the labours of the other three: it inebriates the thirsting soul with the dew of heavenly sweetness.

Reading is an exercise of the outward senses, meditation is concerned with the inward understanding, prayer is concerned with desire, contemplation outstrips every faculty, The first degree is proper to beginners, the second to proficients, the third to devotees, the fourth to the blessed.

13. How these degrees are linked to one another

At the same time these degrees are so linked together, each one working also for the others, that the first degrees are of little use without the last, whilst the last can never or hardly ever be won without the first. For what is the use in spending one's time in continuous reading, turning the pages of the lives and sayings of holy men, unless we can extract nourishment from them by chewing and digesting this food so that its strength can pass into our inmost heart? It is only thus that we can from their example carefully consider our state of soul, and reflect in our own deeds the lives about which we read so often and so eagerly. But how is it possible to think properly, and to avoid meditating upon false and idle topics, overstepping the bounds laid down by our holy fathers (Proverbs 22, 28), unless we are first directed in these matters by what we read or what we hear? Listening is a kind of reading, and that is why we are accustomed to say that we have read not only those books which we have read to ourselves or aloud to others, but those also that our teachers have read to us.

Again, what use is it to anyone if he sees in his meditation what is to be done, unless the help of prayer and the grace of God allow him to achieve it? For 'every good gift and every perfect gift is from above coming down from the Father of lights' (James 1:17): we can do nothing without him, it is he who achieves our works in us, and yet not entirely without us. For we are God's fellow-workers' (1 Corinthians 3:9), as the apostle says. It is God's will, then, that we pray to him, his will that when his grace comes and knocks at our door (Apocalypse 3:20), we should willingly open our hearts to him and give him our consent.

It was this consent that he demanded from the Samaritan

woman when he said: 'Call your husband; (John 4:16); it was as if he said: I want to fill you with grace, and you must exercise your free choice. He demanded prayer from her: 'If you only knew the gift of God, and who he is who says to you, Give me drink, you would perhaps ask him for living waters' (John 4:10). When the woman heard this, it was as if the Lord had read it to her, and she meditated on this instruction in her heart, thinking that it would be good and useful for her to have this water. Fired with desire for it she had recourse to prayer saying: 'Lord, give me this water, that I may thirst no more' (John 4:15).

You can see that it was because she had heard the Lord's word and then meditated on it that she was moved to prayer. How could she have pressed her petition, had she not been fired by meditation? What profit would her meditation have been, if the prayer that followed had not asked for what she had been shown she should desire? From this we learn that if meditation is to be fruitful, it must be followed by devoted prayer, and the sweetness of contemplation may be called the effect of prayer.

14. Some conclusions from what has been said

From this we may gather that reading without meditation is sterile, meditation without reading is liable to error, prayer without meditation is lukewarm, meditation without prayer is unfruitful: prayer when it is fervent wins contemplation, but to obtain it without prayer would be rare, even miraculous. However, there is no limit to God's power, and his merciful love surpasses all his other works; and sometimes he creates sons for Abraham from the very stones (Matthew 3:9), when he forces the hard-hearted and reluctant to comply of their own free will. He acts like a prodigal father, or, as the proverb has it, he takes the ox by the horn when he enters where he has not been invited, when he dwells in the soul that has not sought him. Although we are told that this has occasionally happened, to St Paul for instance (Acts 9), and certain others, yet we ought not to presume that it will, for this would be like tempting God. Rather we should do our part, which is to read and meditate on the law of God, and pray to him to help our weakness (Romans 8:26) and to look kindly on our infirmities. He teaches us this when he says, 'Ask and you will receive, seek and you will find, knock and the door will be opened to you' (Matthew 7:7). For then the kingdom of heaven submits to force, and the forceful take it by storm (Matthew 11:12).

From these definitions you can see how the various qualities of these degrees are linked one with another, and the effects which each one produces in us. Blessed is the man whose heart is not possessed by other concern, and whose desire is always to keep his feet upon this ladder. He has sold all his possessions and has bought the field in which lies hid the longed-for treasure (Matthew 13:44): he wants to be free from all else, and to see how sweet the Lord is (Psalm 46:11; 34:9). The man who has worked in this first degree, has pondered well in the second, who has known devotion in the third, who has been raised above himself in the fourth, goes from strength to strength by this ascent on which his whole heart was set, until at last he can see the God of gods in Sion (Psalm 84:8).

Blessed is the man to whom it is given to remain, if only for a short time, in this highest degree. In truth he can say: now indeed I experience God's face, now with Peter and John upon the mountain I gaze upon his glory, now with Jacob I delight in the embraces of the lovely Rachel. But let such a man beware lest after this contemplation, in which he was lifted up to the very heavens, he plunge violently into the depths, and after such graces, turn again to the sinful pleasures of the world and the delights of the flesh.

Since however the soul has not the power to bear for long the shining of the true light, let it descend gently and in due order to one or other of the three degrees by which it made its ascent; let it rest now in one, now in another, as the circumstances of time and place suggest to its free choice, even though, as it seems to me, the soul is the nearer to God, the further it climbs from the first degree. Such, alas, is the frailty and wretchedness of human nature! In this way, then, we see clearly by reason and the testimony of the scriptures that the perfection of the blessed life is contained in the four degrees, and that the spiritual man ought to occupy himself in them continually. But is there anyone who holds to this way of life? 'Tell us who he is and we will praise him' (Sirach 31:9). There are many who desire it, but few who achieve it. Would that we were among these few.

15. Four obstacles to these degrees

There are commonly four obstacles to these three degrees – unavoidable necessity, the good works of the active life, human frailty, worldly follies. The first can be excused, the second endured, the third invites compassion, the fourth blame. Blame, truly, for it would be better for the man who for love of the world turns his back on the goal if he had never known God's grace, rather than, having known it, to retrace his steps. For what excuse will he find for his sin? (John 15:22). Will not the Lord justly say to him: What more should I have done for you, that I have not done? (Isaiah 5:4). When you did not exist I created you, when you sinned and became the devil's slave I redeemed you, when you were going about with the wicked of this world, I called you away (Isaiah 43:7-11): I let you find favour in my sight, I wanted to make my dwelling with you (John 14:23), and you gave me nothing but contempt: it was not my words alone that you repudiated, it was my own self (Psalm 50:16), and instead you turned away in pursuit of your desires (Sirach 18:20).

But, O my God, so good, so tender and kind, dear friend, wise counsellor, powerful support, how heartless and how rash is the man who rejects you, who casts from his heart so humble and gentle a guest! What a ruinous and wretched bargain to accept evil and harmful thoughts in exchange for his creator, so quickly to throw open the inner chamber of the holy Spirit, that secret place of the heart that so recently echoed with heavenly joys, to unclean thoughts, to turn it into a pig sty (Matthew 7:6). Adulterous desires press in upon the heart where the footprints of the spouse are still plain to be seen. How ill it accords, how unseemly it is for ears which so recently listened to words which man may not utter (2 Corinthians 12:4), so quickly to attend to idle and slanderous stories (2 Timothy 4:4), for eyes so newly purified by holy tears to turn their gaze so soon on worldly vanities, for the tongue which has scarcely ended its song of sweet welcome to the spouse, scarcely has made peace between him and the bride with his burning and pleading eloquence, and has greeted her in the banqueting hall (Canticles 2:4), to revert to foul talk, to scurrility, to lampoons and libels. Never let this happen to us, Lord, and even if we do so fall away through human frailty, never let us despair on that account, but let us hasten back to the merciful leader who lifts up the helpless ones out of the dust, and rescues the poor and wretched from the mire (Psalm 113:7); for he who never desires the death of a sinner (Ezekiel 33:11) will tend us and heal us again and again (Hosea 6:2).

Now is the time for us to end our letter. Let us beseech the Lord together that at this moment he will lighten the load which weighs us down so that we cannot look up to him, and in days to come remove it altogether, leading us from strength to strength through these degrees, until we come to look upon the God of gods in Sion (Psalm 84:7), where his chosen enjoy the sweetness of divine contemplation, not drop by drop, not now and then, but in an unceasing flow of delight which no one shall take away (John 16:22), an unchanging peace, the peace of God (Psalm 4:9).

So, brother Gervase, if it is ever granted to you from above to climb to the topmost rung of this ladder, when this happiness is yours, remember me and pray for me. So, when the veil (Exodus 26) between you and God is drawn aside, may I too see him, and may he who listens say to me also: 'Come' (Apocalypse 22:17).

Liturgical Settings for the Gospels

No	Title	Text	Liturgical Setting
1	Contemplating the Trinity	Jn 14:15-17, 23	6th Sun. Easter(A)
2	Come, Lord Jesus	Mk 13:33-37	1st Sun. Advent (B)
3	Prayer Is Infallible	Lk 11:1-13	17th Sun. (C)
4	Bartimaeus	Mk 10:46-52	30th Sun. (B); 8th Thur.
5	In His Right Mind	Mk 5:1-20	4th Mon.
6	Storm at Sea	Mk 4:35-41	12th Sun. (B); 3rd Sat.
7	Lazarus	Jn 11:1-44	5th Sun. Lent (A)
8	Lenten Conversion	Mt 6:1-6; 16-18	Ash Wednesday
9	A Woman's Conversion	Lk 7:36-50	7th Sun. (C)
10	God, Be Merciful	Lk 18:9-14	30th Sun. (C); 3rd Lent Sat.
11	Come on Down	Lk 19 1-10	31st Sun. (C); 33rd Tues.
12	Do Not Sin Again	Jn 8:2-11	5th Sun. Lent (C)
13	Be Forgiving	Mt 18:21-35	24th Sun. (A); 3rd Lent Tues.
14	An Advent Contemplation	Mt 3:1-12	2nd Sun. Advent (A)
15	Go to Joseph	Mt 1:18-23; Lk 2:1-7	19 Mar; 18 Dec; 4th Sun. Advent (A) Christmas Eve; Christmas Night

No	Title	Text	Liturgical Setting
16	Annunciation to Mary	Lk 1:26-38	25 Mar.; 8 Dec.; 4th Sun. Advent (B); 20 Dec.
17	Our Life of Hope	Lk 2:22-38	2 Feb.; 29 Dec.
18	Jesus Is Baptized	Mk 1:7-11	Baptism of our Lord (B) 6 Jan.
19	Jesus Is Tempted	Lk 4:1-13	1st Sun Lent (C)
20	Jesus Goes Home	Lk 4:16-30	22nd Mon.; Chrism Mass
21	Happy the Poor in Spirit	Mt 5:1-12	4th Sun. (A); 10th Mon.; 1 Nov.
22	The Birds of the Air	Mt 6:25-34	8th Sun. (A); 11th Sat.
23	Feeding of the Multitude	Mk 6:30-44	16th Sun. (B); 4th Sat
24	Who Do You Say I Am?	Mk 8:27-35	24th Sun. (B)
25	You Are the Messiah	Mt 16:13-19	21st Sun. (A)
26	The Transfiguration	Mt 17:1-8	2nd Sun. Lent (A); 6 August (A)
27	Lose Your Life	Mk 8:31-36; 9:33-37	24th Sun. (B); 25th Sun. (C); 7th Tues.
28	Preparing for the Passion	Jn 12:20-30	5th Sun. Lent (B)
29	Gethsemane	Mt 26:31; 36-46	Passion Sunday gospel (part)
30	He Is Risen	Lk 24: 35-48	3rd Sun. Easter (B); 1st Easter Thur.

Liturgical Settings for the Gospels

No	Title	Text	Liturgical Setting
31	Jesus and Mary Magdalene	Jn 20:11-18	1st Easter Tue; 22 July
32	My Lord and My God	Jn 20:24-29	2nd Sun. Easter (A, B, C) 3 July
33	A Great Catch of Fish	Jn 21:1-14	3rd Sun. Easter (C) 1st Easter Fri.
34	I Am The Way	Jn 14:1-14	5th Sun. Easter (A)
35	You Are My Friends	Jn 15:1-17	(1-8) 5th Sun. Easter (B) (9-17) 6th Sun. Easter (B)
36	Life in Abundance	Jn 10:1-10	4th Sun. Easter (A); 4th Easter Mon.
37	Father, Glorify your Name	Jn 17:1-11	7th Sun. Easter; 4th Easter Tue.
38	Safe from the Evil One	Jn 17:11-19	7th Easter Wed.
39	Ascension	Mt 28:16-20	Ascension (A); Trinity (B)
40	Come, Holy Spirit	Acts 1:12-15; 2:1-4	1st reading 7th Sun. Easter (A)
41	Sacred Heart	Mt 11:25-30	Sacred Heart (A); 14th Sun. (A)

www.ingramcontent.com/pod-product-compliance
Lightning Source LLC
Chambersburg PA
CBHW071339080526
44587CB00017B/2896